AGAINST BORDERS

AGAINST BORDERS

The Case for Abolition

Gracie Mae Bradley and Luke de Noronha

VERSO

London • New York

First published by Verso 2022
© Gracie Mae Bradley and Luke de Noronha 2022

1 3 5 7 9 10 8 6 4 2

Verso
UK: 6 Meard Street, London W1F 0EG
US: 388 Atlantic Avenue, Brooklyn, NY 11217
versobooks.com

Verso is the imprint of New Left Books

ISBN-13: 978-1-83976-195-9
ISBN-13: 978-1-83976-196-6 (UK EBK)
ISBN-13: 978-1-83976-197-3 (US EBK)

British Library Cataloguing in Publication Data
A catalogue record for this book is available from the British Library

Library of Congress Cataloging-in-Publication Data

Names: Bradley, Gracie Mae, author. | De Noronha, Luke, 1990– author.
Title: Against borders : the case for abolition / Gracie Mae Bradley and
  Luke de Noronha.
Description: London ; New York : Verso, 2022. | Includes bibliographical
  references.
Identifiers: LCCN 2022005543 (print) | LCCN 2022005544 (ebook) | ISBN
  9781788735803 (paperback) | ISBN 9781788735797 (ebk)
Subjects: LCSH: Boundaries. | Citizenship. | Emigration and immigration. |
  Freedom of movement.
Classification: LCC JC323 .B73 2022 (print) | LCC JC323 (ebook) | DDC
  320.1/2 – dc23/eng/20220325
LC record available at https://lccn.loc.gov/2022005543
LC ebook record available at https://lccn.loc.gov/2022005544

Typeset in Garamond by Biblichor Ltd, Edinburgh
Printed and bound by CPI Group (UK) Ltd, Croydon CR0 4YY

Contents

Introduction

Common-Sense Borders

What do borders do? In conventional accounts, borders establish where one country ends and another begins. They are lines on maps, permanent and taken for granted. Borders delineate a country's territory and mediate the movement of people and goods in and out. They keep out the things that are prohibited: undeclared sums of money, live animals, invasive plant species, disease, drugs – and of course, unauthorised people.

For affluent people in the global North, borders can be crossed with relative ease. There is the brief discomfort of luggage scanners and passport control, before the warm embrace of distant family and the languor of holidays. Law-abiding travellers accept the pat-downs and full-body X-ray scans because they believe that they have nothing to hide – and, indeed, because they share a desire for control, order and safety.

It is this desire for control and security that defines the politics of immigration more broadly: the headlines and political speeches that rail against the dangers of unchecked migration.

Borders are always being breached, it seems. Hence the watery metaphors – the 'deluge', 'waves', or 'floods' of migrants – surpassed only by the animalising language of 'swarms'. Migrants usually come into focus as an assortment of their most threatening characteristics, and the arrival and settlement of migrants – too many, too fast, the wrong type – is seen as bringing only risk, insecurity and national decline.

In this context, governments seem continually compelled to allocate greater resources and more sophisticated technologies to strengthening their borders. The recent rise of right-wing governments has been accompanied by the proliferation of border walls, razor-wire fences, floating barriers in the sea, drones surveilling migrants crossing deserts and oceans, push-backs at the borders of Europe, and the processing of asylum claims in offshore detention camps. The intensification of violent and spectacular bordering is intimately connected to the ascendancy of racist, nationalist and right-wing governments in the present historical moment.[1]

But this is not only a problem on the right. Voices from across the political spectrum assert that borders are sensible and necessary. Many political parties and even trade unions argue that borders protect the working classes from low wages caused by a surplus of migrant labour, ease strains on housing and public services, and preserve the 'way of life' and 'national culture' of migrant-receiving societies. Borders are also said to combat people-smuggling and sex-trafficking, and to prevent the most valuable and talented individuals from abandoning poorer countries. Across these accounts, people on the move are reduced to statistics, units of labour, racialised threats, legal categories and abject victims. Their humanity is effaced, and the 'push factors' driving their decisions to migrate hang in the background: a kind of miasma of war, persecution and ecological collapse divorced from the actions and histories of countries in the global North.

Part of the problem is that the global system of nation-states is simply taken for granted, as if countries and the inequalities between them were natural and permanent. Citizenship – the political/legal system that assigns individuals to states – goes unquestioned. More than this, citizenship is seen as a universal good, a marker of political inclusion and subjectivity, and each individual is supposed to be a citizen 'at home', where they have deep cultural and social ties, and thus where they belong. In this context, immigration controls are seen as merely enforcing coherent legal and spatial distinctions between national populations, through such bureaucratic devices as visas, passports, border checks, and agreements between states. Borders between nation-states are seen to be vital for democracy: they demarcate the necessarily bounded demos.

To sustain this account of borders, all nation-states must be represented as formally equal and sovereign. But this conceit requires a deep historical amnesia about colonialism, and an unwillingness to consider ongoing relations of economic domination. Of course, not all citizenships are equal; citizens of Sweden, New Zealand or the United States have substantially better life chances and greater freedom of movement than citizens of Bangladesh, the Democratic Republic of Congo or

Kyrgyzstan. Immigration controls do not simply carve up the world then, they enforce fixed legal and spatial distinctions between highly unequal nationalised populations.

This book challenges the entire logic of this global order, refusing to accept the world of grossly unequal nation-states. It argues that citizenship and borders, far from protecting democracy and rights, in fact reproduce various forms of inequality, injustice and harm at different scales.

Borders Are Everywhere

The glaring problem with these dominant accounts is that borders are not, in fact, very effective at achieving their stated aims. With or without legal authorisation, the right paperwork, or the right status, people move. Borders may force migrants to take different, longer and more dangerous routes; to use documents in other people's names; and to pay people to facilitate the journey. By depriving people of safer and more direct routes, borders therefore often expose them to harms – robbery, extortion, exploitation and violence – but they do not stop them moving.

And so, people arrive. They make friends, fall in love (with people and with places) and sometimes decide to stay. If they do so without regular status, they might then be excluded from rights to work, to rent housing lawfully, and to access essential public services like health and education. In this context, they are compelled to take jobs within particular sectors, often with particularly bad working conditions, sometimes on pain of criminalisation.

Even migrants with legal status may not have the right to change employer, leave a spouse, or stay after their university course finishes. This limits their ability to express themselves freely, assert rights at work, or leave abusive relationships. Their loved ones may be unable to join or even visit them. Non-citizens may be obliged to submit to regular biometric checks, to pay significant sums to access essential services – on top of other taxes – and to pay lofty fees to maintain their immigration status. Labour migrants, asylum-seekers and undocumented people are often excluded from welfare benefits and free healthcare, even during a global pandemic.

Moreover, as was demonstrated by the so-called Windrush scandal, in which elderly Caribbean migrants in the UK were wrongfully denied access to healthcare and welfare benefits, and in some cases deported to countries they had left in the 1960s and '70s, people can always be deprived of status and rights they have enjoyed for decades.[2]

People who have authorisation to live somewhere might wake up to find the rules have changed, and that they are suddenly 'illegal'. We should not be fooled into thinking of this as an aberration; it is part of what borders do: they follow people around, excluding them in various ways at different times, thus producing the precarity and disposability that characterises the migrant condition.

All of this reminds us that borders do not materialise only at the edges of national territory, in airports, or at border walls. In fact, borders are everyday and everywhere, determining how people relate to partners, employers and the police where they live and work, and their access to healthcare and welfare support.[3]

Borders do not solely affect people on the move, or those who understand themselves to be migrants, but often impact long-settled individuals who have been *illegalised* – turned into migrants – as well as the family and friends of illegalised migrants. More than this, bordering practices have negative consequences for minoritised citizens, who are racialised as 'migrants' or as 'of migrant background' – regularly described as 'second-generation immigrants' despite shared political membership and formal equality (indeed, distinguishing migrants from citizens in multiracial societies is not straightforward).[4] Meanwhile, some non-citizens (migrants in law) are not constructed as migrants in discourse – elite businesspeople, backpackers, and 'expats' are not visible in debates about immigration. Throughout the book we seek to unsettle simplistic oppositions between migrants and citizens, the mobile and the settled. Reality is much messier.

Once we move away from the idea that borders mark the edge of territory, we can see how immigration controls create divisions and hierarchies *within* individual nation-states. Immigration regimes are systems by which differentiated rights are bestowed, and therefore also by which basic rights are denied – such as the rights to work, to join family, to access welfare benefits and healthcare, and to move freely. Borders thus separate workers, neighbours and family members from one another, fuelling racist divisions and nativist resentments. Borders promise to unite citizens through the exclusion of migrants, but this promise proves hollow. Instead, borders are used to surveil and control whole populations, migrants and citizens both, and new forms of disentitlement and conditionality within welfare, education and health services tend to be trialled initially on migrants.[5] Meanwhile, new biometric technologies and predictive analytics are catalysing states' capacities to extend exclusionary and often fatal policing and surveillance practices at borders. None of these techniques will be reserved only for 'migrants'. As we will demonstrate, borders harm us all, which is why we must all be committed to their abolition.

Borders Are New

Immigration controls as we know them are a relatively recent innovation. Before the late nineteenth century, controls on mobility – vagrancy laws, for example – tended to focus on preventing people from leaving state territory, or restricting their movement within domestic space. In 1882, the US government introduced the Chinese Exclusion Act, prohibiting the immigration of all Chinese labourers, and heralding the beginning of modern controls on immigration. In Canada, immigration controls were introduced at the turn of the twentieth century in response to racist resentment towards Indian immigrant labourers.[6] Meanwhile, the 'White Australia' policy effectively prohibited the immigration of all non-European people to Australia – a policy that was backed by all governments and mainstream parties from the 1890s until the 1950s.

Prior to the introduction of immigration controls, the labour needs of these settler colonies had been served by transatlantic slavery, indenture and transportation. Indeed, it was the movement of negatively racialised yet legally free migrants into these territories in the late nineteenth century that seems to have precipitated the introduction of immigration controls. The response to the arrival and settlement of racially undesirable migrants in these settler colonies paved the way for the bordered world we now inhabit.[7]

One way of describing these historical processes is to note that, as states transition from colonial to national forms, they tend to introduce wide-ranging immigration restrictions. This perspective can help us explain the history of British immigration restrictions in the twentieth century, for example. The first immigration restrictions in the UK came with the 1905 Aliens Act, which was explicitly designed to limit the immigration of Jewish migrants escaping persecution in Eastern Europe. But the most significant extension of immigration controls came from 1962 onwards, with the advent of controls on Commonwealth immigrants. After the Second World War, thousands of colonial and Commonwealth subjects moved to the UK from the Caribbean, Africa and South Asia. The racist response from politicians, employers and the general public was intense. In this context, the British government introduced immigration and nationality laws that in effect excluded black and brown Commonwealth subjects from any rights of political membership. The UK defined itself as a nation-state, as an island nation, precisely through the exclusion of people from formerly colonised territories, via the introduction of border controls targeting black and brown colonial and Commonwealth migrants.

Bordered nation-states are thus relatively novel political formations that emerged out of long histories of empire, colonialism and slavery.[8] When we recognise that colonialism 'eats into the present',[9] divisions between territories and populations no longer appear so natural and just. Indeed, borders no longer seem ethically defensible. Most nation-states only became independent after the Second World War; previously, many were colonies of European imperial powers, which explains their global marginality and underdevelopment today. Contemporary borders therefore reproduce racial and colonial inequalities, which helps to explain why bordering practices are most intense precisely at the borders between the developed and underdeveloped world: at the edges of Europe and the southern border of the United States.

Borders Are Obsolete

This book proceeds from a simple point of departure: things do not have to be this way. Immigration controls do not prevent human movement, nor do they protect citizens. In fact, borders produce many of the social harms they claim to prevent, including loss of life, inhuman and degrading treatment, and rampant inequality. Borders fail to address the conditions that shape migration processes in the first place – global inequalities, the dispossession of lands and livelihoods, climate breakdown – and they render people on the move vulnerable to various forms of exploitation and abuse. Immigration controls cannot be used to protect people's rights or to alleviate global inequality; they only ever worsen these problems.

Echoing Angela Davis in her account of prisons, we contend that immigration controls are obsolete and should be abolished.[10] Borders and prisons are both punitive systems for managing undesirable subjects, and both punish people through immobilisation and forced exile. Whatever the important differences between prisons and borders, state violence is in both cases directed towards managing and restricting movement. The struggle for freedom is therefore in both cases a struggle over movement – a struggle for *the right to locomotion*, to move freely, over fences and out of cages.

What we call border abolition is concerned with expanding this freedom, the freedom to move and to stay. This does not mean advocating for free movement in the world as it is currently configured, but rather for transformation of the conditions to which borders are a response.[11] Abolition is concerned with presence (the presence of life-sustaining goods, services and practices of care) as well as absence (of violent state practices like detention and deportation). Accordingly, border abolition seeks to dismantle violent borders, but also to cultivate new ways of caring for one another, nurturing forms of collectivity more conducive to human flourishing than the nation-states we currently inhabit. Border abolition is a revolutionary politics situated within wider struggles for economic justice, racial equality and sustainable ecologies, based on the conviction that there will be no liveable futures in which borders between political communities are violently guarded.

We do not provide a roadmap for how to get to border abolition. We do not know what that world will look like, and there is no single route to get us there. From prison abolition and the wider black feminist politics that shape it, we take a longer-term view of political change. We hope to offer some suggestions and guiding questions, considering the steps we should take and hazards we should avoid. Border abolition offers practical frameworks for acting strategically now, but always focusing on the possibility and urgency of building a world without borders. The first step is to increase our collective understanding of what borders do in the world. This book therefore offers an unflinching account of borders, discussing the connections between immigration control and other forms of state violence and surveillance.

Three broad themes guide our analysis in the chapters that follow. First, abolition requires that we are guided by dreams of a borderless future – our *abolitionist visions*. In the words of Berger, Kaba and Stein, abolition 'is both a lodestar and a practical necessity'. Across the chapters that follow, we attempt to show how the world could be otherwise through an attentiveness to critical openings in the present.[12] Second, our abolitionist framework is concerned with identifying *non-reformist reforms* – changes in the here-and-now that can reduce the power and permanence of borders. Non-reformist reforms offer a way out of the binary opposition between reform and revolution, and help us identify specific reforms in the present that will reduce the power and reach of borders in the short and long term, while avoiding reforms that perpetuate the logic and legitimacy of immigration control (see Chapter 8).

Finally, border abolition requires that we dismantle all the social structures underpinning the permanence of borders, which requires us to connect with wider struggles against connected forms of state violence – something radical activists tend to do much more effectively than those with professionalised roles in the migrant sector. Our invitation to *get out of our silos* – so that people working on issues surrounding migration engage more effectively with feminists, anti-racists, prison abolitionists, people resisting counter-terror policies and those working on issues surrounding tech and data (and, of course, vice versa) – shapes the structure of the book and the arguments it pursues.

Clearly, border abolition is easier said than done. The realisation that the one thing we need to change is everything can certainly be overwhelming.[13] How do we fight to close detention centres and end deportations, stop transnational corporations ruining lives and destroying the planet, while at the same time nurturing spaces of sanctuary and safety in our neighbourhoods? How can we reduce the purview of surveillance, big data and algorithms, while at the same time developing new forms of intimacy beyond the family – all at a time when disaster nationalism seems to be extending its hold over popular political imaginaries? Though the road is long, we should recognise the hopeful signs around us – developments already in motion – and think about the strategies that can build on this work. We need to keep imagining and building, even as despair shadows hope.

In Ernst Bloch's words, 'The work of [hope] requires people who throw themselves actively into what is becoming, to which they themselves belong.'[14] Clearly, this claim chimes with the politics of abolition. Mariame Kaba writes of hope as a discipline, while bell hooks writes that '[h]opefulness empowers us to continue our work for justice even as the forces of injustice may gain power for a time. To live by hope is to believe that it is worth taking the next step.'[15] Hope is not the same as optimism, but rather defined by 'a worldly attentiveness to what is emerging in the conditions of the present as they are carried into the future'.[16] We offer this book as an example of such hope.

We invite you to consider what borders actually do in the world, and to entertain, however briefly, the possibility that communities across the world can relate to one another without recourse to immigration controls. We know that many of you will already share our dreams for a world without borders: for such readers, this book is intended to bolster your resolve, sharpen your critique, and suggest strategies for the long struggle. We are indebted to the radical activists who sustain dreams of revolution, not merely reform, especially in the UK, where we are based: police and prison abolitionists, groups like Corporate Watch, anti-raids networks, No Borders collectives, detainee support groups, and the motley crew of socialists, anarchists, students, queers and community members who show up to protest outside detention centres, chase immigration vans out of neighbourhoods and support illegalised migrants and criminalised populations with innumerable, unremarkable acts of care and solidarity.

That said, this book is written also for people working in NGOs, the legal sector and social services – including radical infiltrators – and is intended to have practical application beyond direct action, mutual aid and other revolutionary schemes. We hope the book will prove useful to those fighting for government policies that are *less bad*, and for more effective NGO campaigning and lobbying. We do not think mutual aid and policy work are mutually exclusive, nor that direct action and NGO campaigns necessarily need to be in conflict.

All of this may be unsurprising given our own biographies. One of us has spent several years working in the NGO sector, as well as being active in grassroots campaigning and abolitionist education initiatives. The other is an academic who teaches and writes about mobilities, borders and racism, but has also written expert reports for UK courts deciding people's immigration cases. We do not pretend to have all the answers, and we have the humility to know that much of what we propose is not new. As Mariame Kaba reminds us, abolition is as much about asking the right questions as having the right answers.[17] Ultimately, we hope this book can open up some space and shed some light for those of us working towards a world without borders and the false promises of race and nation.

I

Race

It's not racist to impose limits on immigration.
Conservative Party 2005 election campaign billboard

All sensible people agree: it is not racist to control immigration. Politicians of various stripes repeatedly proclaim that controls on immigration are necessary, and that they have nothing to do with racism. Racism is morally abhorrent and evil; immigration controls are legitimate and necessary. And yet, every far-right or racist political movement is explicitly anti-immigration and anti-migrant. More generally, the language used to describe unwanted migrants has all the markers of race. People on the move are animalised – think 'swarms' – and depicted as bringers of crime, disease and cultural pathology. And so, states respond by denying people the right to move, settle and access the protections of the law. Migrants starve in deserts, drown in the seas, wallow in detention camps and die of entirely preventable illnesses in nations with supposedly universal healthcare – and apparently none of this has anything to do with race.

In dominant accounts, racism is understood to be an ideology of biological superiority, and racist societies are those where such ideologies are formally encoded into law: the Jim Crow South, Nazi Germany, and apartheid South Africa. Because these political systems no longer exist, and because they are subjects of regret and shame, society is now assumed to be less racist. Indeed, almost everyone agrees that racism is a bad thing, and no one wants to claim it (even fascists and ultra-nationalists mostly claim not to be racist). However, politicians, commentators and dominant institutions from across the political spectrum rarely maintain that racism has been entirely eradicated. They recognise that racist ideas still circulate, but mainly among the ignorant and ill-informed, or in the unconscious biases of the otherwise well-meaning.

Framed in this way, the 'reappearance' of racism is a kind of unfortunate and individualised relapse. Racism is reduced either to individual bigotry and intolerance – which means we must look for the truth of racism in the interpersonal: verbal insults and acts of street violence – or to a question of prejudice within institutions, to be solved with trainings and equality and diversity statements. Racism will go away if only we can correct individual attitudes, and place black and brown people in positions of power within existing institutions.

But racism cannot be reduced to bigotry and prejudice – and race refers to much more than skin colour or biological difference. In fact, we would be better off thinking about race not as a biological fact or a phenotypical marker, but as a system of classification for the management of populations at the global scale, which can draw on biological or cultural referents (and usually both). When we think about the history of the modern world, we can see that race has offered a means of categorising populations so that they can be dispossessed, enslaved and dominated. Ultimately, therefore, what makes a system racial is how groups of people are defined as culturally, geographically and biologically distinct, in order to make them more vulnerable to expropriation, exploitation and uneven development.

From this perspective, it is clear that racism cannot be restricted to Jim Crow, Nazis or apartheid. Race is a system of classification wielded by the powerful to divide humanity in space, in law and in thought. Racism refers to 'the curtailment of life and life's prospects, of social standing and rights, of personal dignity and social possibility because of one's perceived race' – even when that 'perceived race' is not named in terms of skin colour and biology (think of racism targeting Muslims or Gypsy, Roma and Traveller communities).[1] Racism is a 'scavenger ideology' that works through code-words: with reference to Islam, migration, security, civilisation, the European way of life, and the defence of the nation, of women and children, and of liberal values.[2] Importantly for our purposes, it is racism that constructs the settlement of racialised migrants solely in terms of danger, threat and pollution. With this in mind, we can develop more useful responses to the claim: 'it is not racist to control immigration'.

Colonial Modernity, Nationalism and Uneven Mobilities

When politicians assert that immigration policies are not racist, their point is that they do not make any explicit distinctions on the basis of 'race'. Indeed, every nation-state discriminates against foreigners, and so immigration restrictions merely reflect the democratic and sovereign right of a given national population to determine its rules of entry and membership. In other words, immigration controls are not racist – they are simply designed to protect and prioritise the interests of the national community. However, while immigration restrictions might not discriminate on the basis of 'race', they do invariably discriminate on the basis of nationality and poverty. And it is the history of colonialism that has generated the extensive overlap between 'race', nationality and poverty.[3] 'The global poor' maps very closely onto the categories 'formerly colonised' and those racialised as 'non-white', and so border regimes have profoundly racial implications, even as race is 'buried alive'.[4]

The history of the modern world is the history of colonial expansion, domination and dominion: colonialism was 'the darker side of modernity'.[5] As a result, the fact that race, nationality and poverty map onto one another is unsurprising. The modern world was formed through colonialism, and so the nation-states and global inequalities that define the world today cannot be disentangled from race and racism. The world is structured by racial histories and divisions, even if they no longer bear the name 'race'. Indeed, the postcolonial world order is only in its infancy, and therefore carries the weight of centuries of racial domination.

We should also be wary of any attempts to make a neat separation between race and nation, or racism and nationalism. While nationalism might be characterised as reciprocal and non-hierarchical, Western nationalisms in particular have in practice been preoccupied with minorities and outsiders constructed in racial and civilisational terms: Jews, black people, Muslims. As Sivamohan Valluvan explains, 'it is the language and the logic of nation that best hold together a contemporary political discourse that can invoke race but without naming it formally'.[6] For Etienne Balibar,

> the overlapping of [racism and nationalism] goes back to the circumstances in which the nation states, established upon historically contested *territories*, have striven to control *population* movements, and to the very production of the 'people' as a political community taking precedence over class divisions . . . Racism is constantly emerging out of nationalism, not only towards the exterior but towards the interior.[7]

As Balibar explains, nationhood requires the production of a people who belong in a particular territory and have shared destiny despite their obvious class differences. The need to exclude outsiders defined in ethno-racial terms has always been central to this political settlement. When Balibar suggests that '[r]acism is constantly emerging out of nationalism', he encourages us to look for the historically specific ways in which racism and nationalism constitute one another in particular places.

It might be helpful here to discuss a recent and familiar example: Brexit. It was clear that this demand for 'national sovereignty' was inescapably saturated by race. The reactionary populist leader Nigel Farage infamously campaigned by posing in front of a poster that read 'Breaking Point: The EU Has Failed Us'. The poster showed hundreds of brown men – easily read as Muslims – queueing up, presumably to enter Europe, and by extension the UK. It was not clear what this image or the people in it had to do with the UK's membership of the European Union – although the implication was that, once the UK was 'independent' it would gain proper control over its borders. Following the referendum there was a huge spike in racist attacks on the streets and on public transport. Many targeted Eastern Europeans, but black and brown people were also attacked – especially Muslim women. Thus, a national referendum over the UK's political system – its laws, regulations and trade relationships – turned out to be much more viscerally about migrants and minorities, especially those racialised as Muslim. In this way, a political process ostensibly about the demarcation of the nation became inseparable from racist demands for the expulsion of racialised outsiders. Indeed, these two processes always seem to be inseparable.

Since racism and nationalism serve to demarcate a people, excluding outsiders from social and physical space, they are always preoccupied by people on the move. Indeed, people are racialised precisely in terms of how and in what circumstances they move – as in antisemitic tropes of the 'rootless cosmopolitan'; racist expulsions of Gypsy, Roma and Traveller communities; or the intense surveillance and policing of black people in public space. Racism is thus fundamentally preoccupied with space and mobility: who moves, how they move, and who remains where they do not belong.

Relatedly, capitalism has always involved processes of mobilisation and territorialisation, moving and fixing in place. Transatlantic enslavement involved the violent kidnapping and transportation of millions of Africans, followed by their incarceration and subjection on the plantation. Indigenous peoples in North America and Australia have been forcibly contained within particular regions and reservations – forced out, dispossessed, and then fenced in. The camp, the prison and the ghetto all represent sites of immobilisation, and it is precisely this immobilisation that produces and reproduces racial distinctions and hierarchies. As Hagar Kotef explains, 'Through the production of patterns of movement (statelessness, deportability, enclosures, confinement), different categories of subjectivity are produced.'[8] With this in mind, rather than reaffirming the consensus position that migration and migrants create social problems for host communities, we should instead ask, following James C. Scott, 'why the state has always seemed to be the enemy of "people who move around"'.[9]

If racism has always been about legal and spatial exclusion, based on decisions about who gets to move and how, who must be contained and why, then it becomes clear that borders produce racial distinctions and hierarchies in the present – in other words, borders make race, which denotes much more than skin colour, bigotry or prejudice.

When we examine racism through the prism of mobility, we can also see how it changes with time and context. Bordering practices certainly perpetuate colonial inequalities, but they also produce new forms of racial injustice: the refugee camp, the bordering of the seas, and the implementation of enormous biometric databases, for example. Anti-racists need to be alert to how racism shapeshifts, and to how different articulations of racism nourish and reinforce one another. In the British context, we can observe that the demonisation of eastern European migrants since 2004 built upon the anti-asylum politics of the late 1990s and 2000s, all amid a deepening moral panic about Muslim extremism in the context of the War on Terror, and ongoing fears about black youth, serious violence, and 'gangs'. The racialised outsiders change form even as old tropes are repurposed and combined in new ways; our anti-racist politics must therefore nurture connections and coalitions between differently racialised groups – perhaps especially among newly arrived migrants.

For example, the majority of detainees held over recent years in British Immigration Removal Centres are black and brown, many of them nationals of the UK's former colonies; and yet, the top three nationalities deported from the UK have been Romanian, Albanian and Polish since 2016. In this context, differently racialised migrants should not be seen as competitors for meagre privileges, but as people whose shared violation might be the ground for coalitional, radical anti-racist politics. Clearly there is a connection between the young black non-citizens accused of gang affiliation by police, and the Romanian rough-sleepers who are swept up by immigration enforcement teams, both of whom are then detained and deported by the Home Office.

We need to be better at making these connections; it should be impossible for people to think about racism and borders in isolation from one another. The fates of all who are excluded, expelled and caged are intertwined. Communicating this fact requires a historical understanding of how colonialism structures our present, certainly – but also the capacity to identify new articulations of racism and nationalism.

Postcolonial Bordering

If racism and nationalism are inextricable, what does this mean for countries in the global South, in formerly colonised states where the citizenry is not predominantly white? Are borders inherently racist, even in South Africa, India or the Dominican Republic? This might be the wrong question. Whether we call it racism or not, the violent exclusion of people defined as migrants, which then makes it possible to illegalise, detain and deport them, should be of concern wherever it emerges. And so, if we are committed to border abolition as an anti-racist project, racism might not always present itself in the familiar guise of white against non-white.

Throughout the 1960s, most notably in 1969, Ghana expelled to Nigeria hundreds of thousands of 'foreigners' – many of whom were born in Ghana, but were identified as Yoruba. In 1983, the Nigerian government similarly deported approximately 3 million 'foreigners' – many of them to Ghana. Throughout the 1960s, '70s and '80s, such mass expulsions occurred across the African continent, from countries including Sierra Leone, Ivory Coast, Chad, Uganda, Zambia, Kenya, Cameroon, Senegal and Liberia. Since the end of apartheid in South Africa, there has been a sharp rise in anti-immigrant violence, mostly against black people from other African nation-states. In 2002, 250,000 people were expelled from South Africa. In 2011, South Sudan became the world's newest nation-state, and immediately passed a Passports and Immigration Act. Nationality was defined on the basis of historic ties to the land and indigeneity, and many people regarded as southerners were unable to prove that they qualified for membership. They thus became vulnerable to arrest, detention and deportation as 'illegal immigrants'.[10]

Examples like these abound in the process of nation-state formation and war, including the partition of India and Pakistan, population transfers in Cyprus, and the ethnic cleansing of millions of Germans across central and eastern Europe following the Second World War. The list is horrifyingly long. Ultimately, instances of ethnic violence and genocide can be best explained in terms of violent struggles over who is included in the nation and who must be expunged. The Rwandan genocide, for example, emerged from a bitter conflict in which those who were framed as truly native (the Hutus) sought to expunge those who were framed as foreign and colonising (the Tutsis). Ethnic cleansing during the Yugoslav wars involved the targeting of foreign elements considered to be occupying the wrong national homelands. In Myanmar, the Rohingya face a genocide because they are defined as 'illegal Bengali migrants'. Narendra Modi has built his career as prime minister of India on the back of his complicity with anti-Muslim pogroms in Gujarat, and the promise that millions of Muslims will be stripped of their citizenship and interned. The Dominican Republic effectively stripped the citizenship of thousands of Haitian-descended people, which led to instances of mass intimidation, violence and expulsion against those identified as Haitian.

Broadly speaking, the formation of national states has been coterminous with the introduction of immigration controls. Nation-states perform their sovereignty through nationality and immigration legislation, border walls, passports and national identity cards. In the transition from colonial to national states, governments tend to implement immigration restrictions as a kind of rite of passage into nationhood. This applies in the white-settler colonies, which introduced racist immigration and nationality laws at the turn of the twentieth century (Australia, Canada, the United States), as well as in the imperial metropoles of Britain and France, which marked the end of empire in the post-war years with a flurry of restrictive laws designed to exclude former colonial subjects. But it also applies to states across Asia and Africa, which have tended to introduce restrictive immigration and nationality laws very soon after independence.

These processes are not exactly the same, but neither are they totally distinct. When 'national self-determination' justifies controls on immigration in formerly colonised states, we should not romanticise this as a mark of autonomy. After all, borders in newly independent states do not primarily exclude the erstwhile colonisers, but rather penalise migrants from the same region, as well as minorities not seen as autochthonous. These processes of bordering and exclusion are connected to devastating ethnic conflicts in a variety of postcolonial settings.

Of course, ethnic conflicts around the world cannot be explained without an account of colonialism. It is through colonial regimes of rule that the political categories that we currently know as 'native' and 'migrant' were produced and imbued with such fatal significance in the first place.[11] Moreover, these various conflicts over who counts as 'native' and a 'citizen' cannot be explained without considering how the global system creates particular pressures for people in the global South, who have been dispossessed of land – expropriated, exploited and abandoned – and who therefore find political and affective outlets in communitarian movements. Surely the allure of nativism would be lessened if people were able to feed and sustain themselves decently.

We should not comfort ourselves with any suggestion that nationalism is only bad when white people do it. 'White supremacy' will not do all the explanatory work we require of it. Whether violence against migrants and minorities in post-colonial states should be called racism or not is not the main issue. What is important is that the same territorialised, nation-state form is working its deadly magic in new historical contexts.

All of this demands our resistance to nativist politics wherever they flourish. In response to the deadly force of nationalism more generally, we need to nurture forms of political community both beneath and beyond the nation-state. At the local level, this means rejecting nationalism through identification with forms of locality that are more open and tangible. It is no surprise that cities have proved more resistant to anti-immigrant politics than the provinces; indeed, some city municipalities have refused compliance with certain forms of immigration restriction, in some cases declaring themselves cities of sanctuary.

Equally, transnational (or translocal) cultural and political identifications can unsettle the politics of nationalism. Not only BLM in the United States, but also movements like End SARS in Nigeria, have drawn on global connections and sparked concurrent protests around the world. Movements in solidarity with Palestine, Kurdistan, or oppressed groups in India suggest other internationalist and planetary forms of anti-racism and anti-imperialism. These movements recognise shared and connected forms of violation at the hands of the states, particularly in relation to policing and military power. In the very forging of these connections, we create openings towards different worlds – worlds without militarised nation-states. Border abolition should seek to prize open these cracks even further.

Anti-racism and Border Abolition

The now infamous Windrush scandal concerned people who moved from the Caribbean to the UK before 1973, and were caught up in the UK's 'hostile environment' immigration policy: denied access to employment, housing and healthcare, and in some cases deported. As Commonwealth subjects who had moved before 1973, they were entitled to an unconditional right of residence ('right of abode'); but under the 'hostile environment' policy, they became reclassified as 'illegal immigrants'. The public outcry focused on the enforcement of violent borders against the wrong people. Politicians and commentators of all stripes repeated the claim that these individuals were citizens – not illegal immigrants.

Labour MP David Lammy wrote a short piece in the *Guardian* referring to the Windrush generation as 'citizens' no less than ten times. As he explained, this scandal was about 'citizens who have been treated like criminals in their own country'. In this way, the harm done to Windrush migrants was isolated from the treatment of more recent migrants who were impacted by the hostile-environment policy – people who were also illegalised, forced into destitution, detained and deported. The resolution to the scandal was thus to be found in redress for the Windrush migrants alone, rather than in a total overhaul of the system that denies non-citizens access to the basic means of life – in other words, an end to the hostile environment.

In general, campaigns for citizenship for particular groups of migrants function to reinforce the notion that you have to be a particular kind of person – a citizen, an insider, someone who belongs – in order to access fundamental rights. This is a reformist demand insofar as it does nothing to undermine the assumption that only citizens can make claims on the state: claims to basic rights, dignity and freedom from coercion. Non-reformist demands would call for rights for non-citizens – for the establishment of the non-citizen as a person with rights against the state – potentially recuperating the long-unfulfilled promise of human rights. This would mean that access to rights would no longer be predicated on citizenship status, which has increasingly been constructed as a 'privilege' in the context of the War on Terror.

In short, we argue that anti-racism should centrally include people subject to immigration controls (non-citizens), without trying to resolve the problem by simply turning them into citizens. This does nothing to challenge the logic of exclusion, or to protect the wider population of people excluded from membership. As people committed to border abolition, we need to ask: What lies beyond citizenship?

When anti-racists ignore the mutually constitutive nature of racism and nationalism, they become reconciled to the nation, and seek redress for racism within its comfortable confines. This often means seeking representation within its dominant institutions. In its crudest form, this might mean celebrating the fact that the current UK government is the most ethnically diverse yet, with black and brown faces in high (authoritarian) places. But it is also visible in various calls for diversity in boardrooms, police departments and elite universities. Clearly, black and brown bosses, billionaires and police chiefs will not help the majority of black and brown people whose lives are diminished by racial and class oppression. We should also recognise that demands for diversity in institutions like universities and large NGOs can function to displace and silence more radical demands for changes to the structure and strategies of these institutions – and even their potential dismantling and the redistribution of their resources. The banal politics of representation works as a distraction: a campaign for a black woman to be put on a banknote, for example.

Of course, there are many anti-racist initiatives that do important work while still operating within the confines of the nation. Groups challenging institutional racism tend to focus on what we might call second-class citizenship: the ways in which racialised citizens are excluded and discriminated against despite their formal membership. Some of these anti-racist programmes help all people subject to racism, including non-citizens; but immigration controls are usually not part of the picture. Problems arise when we assume that racism is about inequalities *between* citizens, even when we know that many racialised people in the UK are denied citizenship. So, while we fight against structural racism in schools, workplaces, and the healthcare and criminal justice systems, we should also recognise that borders exclude people from accessing education, employment, free healthcare and fundamental rights to due process in the first place. We must avoid playing into the idea that racism is bad because it 'divides the nation' or 'excludes citizens', as though we all agree that citizenship is a good thing, and support the ideal of full and equal membership only for the nation's insiders.

Anti-racists must seek the abolition of borders. People campaigning for racial equality should be struggling against all immigration controls, just as migrants'-rights advocates should be thinking about the weight of racism in determining their impacts. We can learn from black freedom struggles that freedom from racism means the freedom to move unchained – emancipation being inseparable from the right to locomotion.

In pursuit of border abolition, we need to cultivate alternative ways of imagining collectivity beyond and against race and nation. We would do well to remember that modern ways of thinking about peoplehood, identity and territory are fairly new, and that their hold over us is never total. As we become increasingly conscious of our shared vulnerability to climate change and global pandemics, we urgently need to develop planetary sensibilities and a commitment to a world held in common. Abolishing borders must be central to this project, a global fight with many sites of struggle.

Migrant activists in Europe rightly seek to challenge the EU's violent border regime and secure people's safe passage by any means necessary. But border abolition also means ensuring that Africa, for example, becomes a space of free movement. As Achille Mbembe puts it, 'If we want to conclude the work of decolonisation, we have to bring down colonial boundaries in our continent and turn Africa into a vast space of circulation for itself, for its descendants and for everyone who wants to tie his or her fate with our continent.'[12]

Ultimately, we need to dismantle borders and walls wherever they have been built: between India and Bangladesh, Israel and Palestine, Saudi Arabia and Iraq, the United States and Mexico. Borders scar both the land and our political imaginaries: the hopes of dispossessed people must never be for their own territory and their own fortress. By thinking about the problem of racism and borders from the perspective of formerly colonised populations, we can see that the deeper problem is the territorialisation of land, peoples and cultures, and their transformation into national property. This reckoning with the inherently exclusive nature of the nation-state demands that we develop alternative political forms and ideas about movement, land, culture and difference.

2

Gender

Today, immigration law still promotes sex and childbearing within marriage, endlessly reproducing both heteropatriarchy and classes of immigrants who face exclusion for nonreproductive sexuality or childbearing outside marriage, or childbearing within marriage that costs the state money.

Eithne Luibhéid, *Entry Denied: Controlling Sexuality at the Border*

Sham Marriage: Who Counts as a Spouse?

A camera crew follows immigration enforcement officers as they interrupt a 'sham marriage'. In the middle of a low-key civil ceremony, agents intervene to prevent the 'immigration offender', a Pakistani national, from marrying the 'fake bride', a Slovakian national. The man is put in handcuffs and arrested, while the woman is interviewed to determine whether she was marrying for cash or was in fact duped by a fake romance. The details and the locations vary, but the stories are much the same. BBC News, Sky News, Channel 5 and other outlets filmed similar shocking exposés in the early 2010s, forming part of a moral panic about so-called sham marriages. These stories were not only about migrants cheating the system; they focused on the abuse of the institution of marriage.

In immigration law, as in civil law more broadly, primacy is given to marriage. Marriage is a way to make one's relationship legible to the state. For non-citizens seeking rights, marriage can be an important avenue for claims-making. In British immigration law, people on certain visas can apply to bring dependents – spouses and children, for example – while other non-citizens can make immigration applications on the basis of relationships with spouses resident in Britain (although the Home Office has made it difficult to 'switch visas' – for a temporary worker to switch to a spousal visa, for example). Migrants who are not married can still make claims to family life with a 'qualifying partner' (usually a citizen), but this must be shown to be a relationship 'akin to marriage' – which means cohabitation, shared financial responsibility and, of course, monogamy.

Clearly, marriage remains the ideal, and something that must be protected. Indeed, it is because some people apparently use marriage to secure their stay that marriages involving non-citizens are subject to inspection and surveillance. Hence all the shocking sting operations revealing the scourge of 'sham marriages'. As a result, non-citizens now need to receive clearance before they wed, surveilled from the beginning.

Since 2012, the UK government has stipulated that British citizens must earn at least £18,600 a year if they want to bring a non-EU spouse to live in the UK (requiring another

£3,800 for a first child, and £2,400 for each subsequent child). This effectively prevents people on minimum wage from bringing their foreign spouses to the UK, and has particularly marked effects for women, especially ethnic minority women. Put bluntly, 'it is virtually impossible for unemployed or disabled people on benefits to marry a person from outside the EU'.[1] Around the same time, the British government extended the probationary period for spouses from two years to five years, apparently 'to test the genuineness of the relationship'.[2] This means that if a couple splits within those five years, the migrant spouse does not have the right to claim settlement independently. Unsurprisingly, this has had the effect of trapping migrant spouses in unhappy and sometimes abusive relationships, where they are effectively dependent on their citizen spouse for their residence. Leaving a relationship means becoming undocumented, and potentially facing deportation.

People on spousal visas in the UK are usually subject to a policy that stipulates they have 'no recourse to public funds', which means that they cannot legally claim welfare benefits – including Disability Allowance, Housing Benefit, out-of-work benefits and Child Benefit. This makes migrant spouses especially dependent on their sponsoring partners, because they will be rendered destitute if they exit relationships. The exclusion of non-citizen spouses from social rights, combined with the threat of deportation, thus creates the conditions for abuse. Thus, one key non-reformist demand would be to ensure that such migrants can claim rights independently of a spouse (and indeed of an employer), so that everyone has a means of exiting situations of domestic abuse or workplace exploitation.

Abolitionist demands focus on reducing the reach and force of immigration enforcement – which in this case extends into people's intimate and family lives. That means less surveillance, inspection and conditionality surrounding marriages, as well as the extension of rights to individuals independent of their relationships to spouses. More ambitiously, it means dethroning the marriage relation altogether by allowing people to move and access rights without laying their intimate and personal lives out for bureaucratic scrutiny.

Reproducing the Nation: Who Counts as a Parent?

In 2018, Donald Trump courted further notoriety when he separated thousands of migrant children from their parents. He introduced a 'zero-tolerance' policy towards undocumented arrivals, subjecting border-crossing parents to criminal prosecution for their 'illegal entry' – and then detaining their children separately as 'unaccompanied minors'. A former Walmart in Texas was converted into a detention centre for thousands of immigrant children, while their parents faced criminal prosecution. These practices caused widespread outrage and consternation, as images of groups of children sleeping on floors in cages circulated online. These practices were horrifying by any measure, but what made them resonate particularly strongly were dominant ideas about children, parents and the family.

Indeed, these practices were seen as morally wrong even under the terms of restrictionist immigration policy: you are not supposed to separate families and lock up innocent children as a matter of course. Indeed, immigration law recognises the importance of relations between parents and children –

albeit mostly defined biologically. Clearly this is a good thing; many people's relationships with their children are those most precious and deeply valued. The question for border abolition, however, concerns what kinds of relationship are made invisible when biological relationships between parents and children are afforded primacy – even if they are, in practice, still routinely disregarded.

Part of the tension here is that the special concern for children usually affords only very limited rights to those who care for them, most often mothers. Fathers are regularly deported despite any responsibilities they may have in caring for children, usually because it is imagined the mother's care is more important. Meanwhile, for mothers, the flipside to the recognition that they are responsible for bearing and raising children is that their motherhood then becomes something to be policed and controlled. Migrant women are regularly accused of cynically bearing children to gain rights – and, as always, racism determines whose motherhood becomes a problem. For example, while progressives in Ireland proudly celebrate the referenda that legalised gay marriage and abortion, it is often forgotten that in 2004 around 80 per cent voted to end birthright citizenship, in direct response to a moral panic about black and brown asylum-seeking women gaining rights through their citizen children born in Ireland.[3] Similar ideas underwrite debates about so-called 'anchor babies' and the 14th Amendment to the US Constitution.

Margaret Thatcher abolished birthright citizenship in the early 1980s, and Britain continues to stigmatise and punish migrants who have children. Illegalised migrants in Britain now face an average bill of around £7,000 for an uncomplicated childbirth. Troublingly, this now means that the

National Health Service is tasked with charging migrants and reporting them to immigration authorities if and when their bills go unpaid. Charges within the NHS were expanded under Britain's hostile-environment immigration policy, and have had predictably racialised and gendered implications. Of course, attempts to control, police and punish the fertility of migrants reflect broader concerns surrounding demographic shifts, in which anti-immigrant voices warn that white majorities are being replaced by non-white migrants (especially Muslims). Who has babies, at what rate, and what kind of rights they are entitled to are matters of great concern to racists and nativists, and immigration controls are seen as the nation's principal line of defence. For this reason, the sexual and reproductive lives of migrant women become a key target of immigration control.

The Limits of 'Family Life'

In September 2016, the UK government chartered a mass deportation flight to Jamaica, and began rounding up Jamaican nationals from their homes, from prisons and at reporting centres. Most had been here for many years, and many made last-ditch appeals against their expulsion. Darel had six children. For four of them, he was the primary carer – he made them breakfast, took them to school, and picked them up each day. He appealed against deportation on these grounds. Michelle argued that her relationship with her partner of several years made her deportation disproportionate. She also acted as a carer for her own mother. Michael appealed his deportation because he had been living in Yorkshire since he was two years old, his entire family was in the

UK. He knew no one in Jamaica. However, despite their protestations, Darel, Michelle and Michael were all deported on the flight, along with another thirty-nine Jamaican nationals.[4] Their claims to family life were not deemed important enough to outweigh the 'public interest' in their deportation.

Michelle was unable to stay in the UK partly because the children she cared for were not her biological children – her role as step-parent was not enough. Darel's separation from his children was not regarded as 'unduly harsh' either, despite him being their primary carer. Meanwhile, Michael was unable to articulate the significance of his relationships with his cousins, his aunties and his grandmother – which were effectively meaningless under immigration law: the special weighting given to the 'wellbeing' of children is accompanied by the total disregard for relationships between adult family members, including between adults and their parents. And what about friends? Among those deported on the charter flight were several young single men with criminal records, many in their late teens and early twenties. Friendship can be the most important form of connection for people in this sit-uation, as it can for all of us; and yet such ties are often framed as 'gang associations' rather than as friendships defined by mutual support and care.

Darel, Michelle and Michael all had family connections in the UK, but they were not recognised as valid or valuable – which is routine for migrants who commit crimes, claim benefits, sell sex, use drugs or live in households that are not nuclear families. But the broader question remains: Why is being part of a family necessary for claiming rights and protections?

While life under capitalism individualises and atomises us, we are still governed through the logics of the family. We seem unable even to think about or describe nation-states without deferring to metaphors of the family: the mother- or fatherland; the family of nations; the homeland. Like families, nations get to welcome people in, or refuse people entry and membership; they are bounded and necessarily exclusive. The nation is imagined as one big family, but also as an entity made up of families. It is worth remembering that Margaret Thatcher's much cited claim that there is no such thing as society was followed immediately by: 'there are individual men and women *and there are families*' (our emphasis). The institution of the family – the monogamous, nuclear, heterosexual family, that is – is seen as guarding against atomisation, disorder, and anomie, providing a moral framework for the nation.

Hence the provisions in UK immigration law to safeguard 'the best interests of the child', and to recognise 'genuine and subsisting' relationships between partners (especially spouses). And yet, people with British partners and children are regularly deported precisely because their 'private and family life' is not seen to be proper or normative – and thus not compelling enough to prevent family separation.

In fact, the overarching concern for 'family life' is encoded into international human rights law. Article 16(3) of the Universal Declaration of Human Rights states: 'The family is the natural and fundamental group unit of society and is entitled to protection by society and the State.'[5] Article 8 of the European Convention of Human Rights states: 'Everyone has the right to respect for his private and family life, his home and his correspondence.'[6] These rights raise more questions than they answer: What kind of family? What makes it natural? And what does a home look like?

There is a tension here for liberal states. As we know, contemporary nation-states are concerned with controlling immigration and restricting the rights of non-citizens. They are therefore anxious to restrict the rights of people who might enter and settle by means of family and marriage connections. However, liberal states cannot ignore rights to 'family life' altogether. Instituting a blanket ban on citizens marrying foreigners, for example, would be widely regarded as an extreme and illiberal policy. In an attempt to resolve these tensions, states seek to delimit whose family life counts, thus restricting access to these rights. In this process of determining what 'proper' relationships with children, partners and employment should look like, states reinforce normative ideas about gender and sexuality.

Relationships to a spouse, a monogamous partner or children under the age of eighteen might capture the most important forms of intimacy and care for many people; but for many others they might not. And why should they? What about the families we choose? Our friends and comrades, our kith as well as our kin? Immigration controls would fall apart if there were such a thing as a friendship visa, which tells us something important about what is to be gained by valuing a wider range of intimacies. In 2011, then home secretary Theresa May claimed that an 'illegal immigrant' had avoided deportation because of his relationship to his cat. This was patently untrue – simply part of May's rhetoric on 'soft-touch' Britain (note the gendered implications of the word 'soft'). But, in any case, would we not want to live in a world where a person's relationship to their cat means something? And what about our individual, intrasubjective relationships to places and memories? To avoid deportation, we must prove the strength of our relationships to knowable others (for now, restricted to humans); but we might want to remain in a place for no reason other than because it is familiar and we like being there.

There is a cautionary point here. While fighting for reforms, we might ask the state to recognise a wider variety of family structures; but this entails the risk that, in asking the state to validate more kinds of relationship, we grant it access to – and power over – a more extensive and detailed map of people living non-heteronormative lives. Already, determinations over sexuality in asylum claims, and in claims relating to family and private life, are incredibly invasive in their attempts to know and assess the quality and character of people's intimate relationships (degrading and graphic questions about the sex lives of queer asylum applicants provide only the most obvious example here). Those of us working towards border abolition should do so on the basis that people should be able to move and be free from the threat of deportation without having to offer up an intimate picture of their private lives. Again, this means that our principal strategy should be to reduce the state's power to surveil, detain and deport, while also expanding the scope of the rights under which people can move – for example, by reducing and abolishing forms of conditionality and dependency.

Domestic and Sex Work: Who Counts as a Worker?

Migrant women are often compelled to claim rights as wives, mothers and/or victims. But clearly many women migrate for primarily the same reason as men – to work. However, the ability of women to claim rights as workers is often profoundly restricted. This is because the sectors in which they predominate are often not considered 'proper' work, especially in relation to domestic and sex work.

Feminists have long written about how women's work in the home is naturalised, demeaned and undervalued, and wives/mothers are simply expected to do it all. Domestic work is constructed as care work, a 'labour of love'; it happens in the home, the private sphere, and so is not subject to the formal relations of the labour market.[7] But what happens when poorer, usually racialised, women are employed to do this work? As Bridget Anderson notes, 'foreignness can help employers and host families manage their deep discomfort around the introduction of market relations into the home'.[8] For migrant domestic workers, the employment relation is marked by tensions around what counts as work and what counts as care, and a blurring of employment and family relations.

Live-in migrant domestic workers are often considered 'part of the family' in ways that prove most beneficial to employers. After all, overtime is not really overtime when the host family *care about you*, and might be doing you a favour by employing you as a desperate and poor third-world woman. Migrant domestic workers are often excluded from national minimum wage and other labour market protections, partly because of this blurriness around work and care, public and private. Policies vary in different states, but for many live-in domestic workers, visas are tied to specific employers, which creates the conditions for extreme forms of exploitation and abuse. This has been a key site of struggle for migrant domestic workers around the world.

In the 1990s in the UK, migrant domestic workers, working with the wider trade union movement, campaigned for the right to change employers. They campaigned to be treated as independent workers, rather than members of the family. The problem was that migrant workers in general were not allowed to change employers. Migrant domestic workers therefore were not asking to be treated like other migrant workers, but for exceptional rights on the basis of their vulnerability to physical abuse and exploitation in the home. This was extremely successful, and in 1998 migrant domestic workers won the right to change employers. A campaign for all migrant workers would certainly have been much harder to win, but the problem with these campaigns was that they often traded on the same images of brutalised migrant women and barbaric foreign employers, who were usually portrayed as Middle Eastern. In other words, rights were granted not because domestic labour was a job like any other, but because it was not.[9]

Fourteen years later, in 2012, the Coalition government once again stripped domestic workers of their right to change employer. Clearly this was bad news. The organisation Kalayaan found that abuse of various kinds was roughly twice as prevalent among people on tied visas than among those who could change employers. After 2012, migrant domestic workers could only exit their employment legally if they were identified as victims of 'modern slavery'. In practice, this meant making oneself visible to the police and the Home Office, and not everyone who is referred through the National Referral Mechanism is recognised. Indeed, being identified as a (potential) victim is no guarantee of protection from illegality, detention and deportation in the long run.

In this context, there is a need for further campaigning to reinstate the right of migrant domestic workers to change employers – like that being done by Kalayaan and others. A key question, however, concerns whether and how such a demand might be integrated into a wider campaign to end all forms of tied visa. If we recognise that abolitionist demands may exceed the tempo of the latest news or election cycle, then we need to fight to end all forms of dependency within immigration control and explode the categories which define non-citizens solely in terms of their labour power.

People committed to border abolition should also join calls to decriminalise sex work. Migrants who sell sex face multiple obstacles when seeking to get away from situations of extreme exploitation and violence, due to the criminalisation of both their work *and* their migration statuses. Juno Mac and Molly Smith put it clearly:

> For [migrant] sex workers, the solution includes dismantling immigration enforcement and the militarised border regimes that push undocumented people into the shadows and shut off their access to safety or justice – in other words, taking power away from the police and giving it to migrants and to workers.[10]

Mac and Smith convincingly argue that the main source of vulnerability for migrant sex workers is precisely their vulnerability to deportation and police power. While some feminists remain preoccupied with the act of buying and selling sex, emphasising the abject suffering of particular sex workers and the misogyny and entitlement of clients, Mac and Smith explain that migrant sex workers can be best supported through decriminalisation and an end to violent immigration controls. Borders prevent people from moving, seeking legal employment, and from accessing social rights, which makes sex work one of the only means of survival for many illegalised migrants, a sector which is itself criminalised. As Mac and Smith remind us, solutions focused on more laws, more police, and more immigration restriction always fail migrants who sell sex.[11]

Empowerment Not Victimhood

Thinking about gender is not the same as thinking about women. Nevertheless, in many liberal strains of migrant activism, campaigns are organised around a sense that immigration controls are bad because they are bad for women in particular. For example, there has been more campaigning and media coverage around Yarl's Wood Immigration Removal Centre, which holds most female detainees, than any other detention centre in the UK . Yarl's Wood is infamous for good reason: there have been repeated reports of sexual abuse by staff, huge solidarity protests have been organised outside the centre, and groups of detained people have themselves organised political actions and hunger strikes. While the people organising these actions have steadfastly demanded that all detention centres be shut down, for much of the broader audience Yarl's Wood is the only immigration detention centre they have heard of. Much of the media coverage of Yarl's Wood focuses on women who have experienced rape and sexual violence. The trauma and suffering of the women involved then provides a basis for them to claim rights.

The danger here is that women in Yarl's Wood become victims to be rescued, rather than people working towards their own freedom. Images of black and brown women as abject victims seem to have a stubborn appeal for liberal white feminists, in ways that render the prevalence of experiences of rape and sexual violence among men and gender non-conforming people invisible. There is a kind of gender exceptionalism at play here that can prove harmful in the wider struggle against borders. But we can look to the demands of women on hunger strike in Yarl's Wood in February 2018 for a different way forward.[12]

The Yarl's Wood hunger strikers demanded access to justice, an end to indefinite detention, better healthcare, an end to charter flights, and an end to people being re-detained. They did not limit their demands to Yarl's Wood, and referred to 'people' rather than 'women'. They made specific demands that survivors of rape should not be re-traumatised through detention; they also protested about how LGBTQ+ people were being disbelieved and hormone treatment was being discontinued for some trans detainees. They demanded that families should not be separated, and that those who had come to the UK as children and/or had been in the country for ten years should be given amnesty. All these demands would have benefited the large majority of immigration detainees who are men, who were facing the same conditions and the same crushing threat of forced removal.

This shows that it is possible to make claims from the perspective of people who are multiply oppressed in ways that move towards greater freedom for everyone. This has been the gift of black feminism. Where white liberal feminism is motivated by charity, humanitarianism and rescue, black feminism emphasises collective liberation and emancipation. Unsurprisingly, it is the liberal politics of rescue that has proved especially state-friendly, most apparent today in policies that seek to combat trafficking and modern slavery.

The global rise in statements and policies targeting 'trafficking' and 'modern slavery' has gone hand in hand with increasingly violent, draconian and globe-spanning measures to combat 'illegal immigration'. At the centre of 'anti-trafficking' work is a carceral and punitive logic in which states are forces for good, saving goodies from baddies. As Bridget Anderson puts it, 'trafficking seems to be a rare patch of common ground between NGOs, activists, and states'.[13] For this reason, we must keep arguing and showing that it is borders that render people vulnerable to particular kinds of abuse, by illegalising non-citizens, forcing them to take risky and unprotected journeys, which often entails accruing debts, and compelling undocumented migrants to earn a living in informal and criminalised economies (note, migrants who sell drugs and migrants who sell sex are bound by similar forces, although in differently gendered ways).

The problem is that, under the name of combating trafficking and slavery, the border acquires renewed legitimacy, to the detriment of those who are putatively being rescued. When immigration authorities raid places where 'trafficked' and 'enslaved' people are suspected to be working and living, for example, they almost always find more immigration offenders than victims: rescue missions strongly resemble enforcement sweeps. Moreover, the logic of trafficking and slavery dictates that violent individual men – those swarthy traffickers – must be deported. But, as prison abolitionists have shown us, the vast majority of gendered and intimate violence is not visible to or even taken seriously by the state. Even in cases where men have abused women, imprisoning and then deporting them does not offer an effective remedy. It merely erases and outsources the problem – in the case of deportation, to another national territory.

There remains a tension here in terms of political strategy. While we should be extremely wary about the languages of trafficking and slavery, they do offer some legal avenues for people who have few other options. As Ava Caradonna explains,

> For migrants the question of work, to undertake any work, is often considered the most heinous crime against the state that we can commit. If we are caught in the act of working, our best immediate survival strategy is to argue that we were NOT working and that we were in fact coerced. To put it simply, if you are defined as a trafficked woman then you have some rights and access to resources, if you are defined as a migrant sex worker you don't.[14]

This is a perennial problem for those seeking non-reformist reforms: How do we make radical demands without letting the state strip away existing, even if inadequate, protections?

We do not profess to have all the answers. But we do know that, in the long run, we need to move away from gendered narratives of victimhood, suffering and rescue.

Wherever possible, we should avoid playing into and thereby legitimising the languages and policies of 'modern slavery' and 'trafficking' that seem to serve restrictionist states so well. Instead, we should seek to make broader claims. Migrants living and working with precarious statuses show us the way, often by making claims as 'workers'. The insights of sex-worker campaigns can be applied to migrant struggles more broadly: end the criminalisation of work and stop police and immigration raids. These immediate and simple demands, while radical, offer the best promise of protections and increased freedom for all criminalised and illegalised people.

Ultimately, if we want to abolish borders, we need to explode the legal categories that restrict access to rights and protections (and exploding categories is quintessentially queer, when we understand queerness, following bell hooks, 'as being about the self that is at odds with everything around it and has to invent and create and find a place to speak and to thrive and to live').[15] Each person is always more than a 'worker', a 'spouse' or a 'refugee', and migrants' rights advocates need to maintain a critical distance from these legal classifications. Deportation is wrong not simply because it destroys families, but because forcible expulsion itself is fundamentally objectionable. Detention is unjust not simply because survivors of torture are among the detainees, but because incarcerating people is itself a form of torture. The limited categories of deservingness within immigration law have distinctly gendered implications. As people try to make themselves legible as proper 'spouses', 'parents' and 'victims' of persecution, gendered ideas about vulnerability, dependency and lack of agency are reproduced. Clearly, we do not want to do away with all of these categories tomorrow, however limited the protection they offer. But it is by centring the struggles of people excluded from the categories of 'worker', 'spouse' and 'victim' – queers, sex workers, even 'gang members' – that we can best develop radical demands and identify abolitionist reforms.

3

Capitalism

What Is Capitalism?

Free immigration is just free trade applied to labor.
Bryan Caplan, author of *Open Borders:*
The Science and Ethics of Immigration

If borders were open: A world of free movement would be $78 trillion richer.

Economist

For the likes of the *Economist* and the World Bank, and for commentators like Bryan Caplan, debates about 'open borders' tend to hinge on whether migration is good for 'economic development'. They ask questions like: Does migration increase overall productivity, and how can we ensure that migration works both for the countries that receive migrants and the countries that send them? This kind of economistic thinking underpins dominant policy approaches to 'managed migration', which seek to advance the national economies of receiving states and to foster 'development' in sending societies. Some argue that free movement can increase the efficiency and productivity of markets, which is an argument not for the free movement of people, but for the free movement of (rightless) labour. It is also noted that migrants send remittances back home, which aids development. But the first question we need to ask is: What do we mean by 'development'? And why is no one questioning the vast inequalities between national populations in the first instance? For free-market proponents of migration, 'development' means capitalist development, and thus the prioritisation of profit over people. Clearly, border abolition needs to be distinguished from these arguments for 'open borders', and this requires a more critical account of the relationship between capitalism and immigration control.

Capitalism is an economic system in which people can own private property and exchange goods and services in the marketplace in pursuit of their own rational self-interest. For its proponents, capitalism produces the best outcomes in terms of overall wealth, prosperity and growth, while ensuring personal, private freedoms and facilitating the most efficient distribution of goods and services. The role of liberal-capitalist states and international organisations under this system is to protect the rights of private citizens and maintain an orderly environment for the proper functioning of markets.

For capitalism's critics, especially Marxists, dominant conceptions of equal exchange in the marketplace obscure material relations of production and the exploitation of dispossessed wage workers. Capitalists own the means of production, and their profits accrue from the difference between how much value is produced by labour and what workers are paid. Capitalism produces vast and widening inequalities between those who own the means of production – capitalists – and everyone else. As a global system, capitalism requires constant growth; new markets must be prized open and expanded. Everything must be commodified; this is why, for the global majority, the goods that are necessary for basic survival – food, water, shelter, electricity and so on – are things we have to pay for. Thus, the global majority, who have been dispossessed of their means of self-reproduction and subsistence, are compelled to sell their labour-power – that is, to be exploited – or to hustle in informal labour markets. The role of states in this system is to ensure the smooth functioning of capital accumulation (otherwise known as profit-making), and to reproduce consent for domination among the oppressed classes (often referred to as hegemony).

Of course, capitalism is not static through time and space: early industrial capitalism in the north of England worked very differently to the gig economies of the twenty-first century. Likewise, the influence of sugar planters and insurance companies at the high point of the transatlantic slave trade is not equivalent to the role of property developers and derivatives traders in contemporary megacities – even though both have shaped the global capitalism of their time. However, capitalism in all its forms relies on the production and management of differences between groups of people – especially racial, national and gendered differences (readers will note that the three chapters on capitalism, racism and gender necessarily overlap). Thus, capitalism is and always has been geographically uneven, producing and exaggerating racialised distinctions and hierarchies.

Marx wrote about how early capitalist development relied upon the violent dispossession of people's land, rendering them propertyless and therefore leaving them no choice but to sell their labour-power (a process he called primitive accumulation). In the English context, this involved the enclosure of the commons – the removal of communal rights to access and use land, and its appropriation as private property reserved for the sole use of landowners or their tenants. But in a global perspective, the conditions of possibility for capitalist development involved conquest, genocide and enslavement. For example, the global production of sugar, tobacco and cotton relied on first seizing the lands of peoples in the Americas, and later kidnapping and enslaving millions of Africans to work in bondage to produce valuable commodities for global markets. In other words, theft, murder, conquest and plunder made the world of free markets, exchange, wage labour and private property, and these world-making processes continue to shape the geography of racialised global inequality today.

Of course, we now live in a postcolonial world in which formal racial rule is considered illegitimate, and where the explicit legislation of racial difference and hierarchy has mostly been abolished. However, the world made by colonialism has not been transformed or repaired, and racial and national disparities still characterise the distribution of life chances in an increasingly unequal world. Despite many successful struggles for formal rights and recognition, the structural inequalities forged by colonialism remain, mediated more indirectly by immigration controls and restrictive citizenship regimes. This is one of the ways in which we might describe our contemporary world order as racial, or racist: the borders between nation-states perpetuate hierarchies made by colonialism.

Importantly, these racialised global inequalities are maintained by the contradiction between the mobility of capital and the immobility of labour. Capital seeks to overcome restrictive national protections that prevent the accumulation of profit. Thus, large corporations – mostly founded in and operating from the global North – insist on access to the natural resources of southern countries (mining companies, for example), and demand the ability to sell products in their local markets (manufactured goods, food products, financial services, and so on). In this way, capital is enabled to move (relatively) freely, pursuing a kind of borderlessness denied to humanity. Of course, there is nothing natural about this world order: capital moves easily precisely because powerful states, corporations and international organisations have forcibly removed regulations, tariffs and protections that might protect local economies and modes of subsistence in the global South. These processes are central to what is called 'neoliberalism'.

Meanwhile, labour is contained, and the global majority are immobilised in places of relative scarcity. Importantly, this contradiction is justified through ideas about national, racial and cultural difference. Mythologies around race and nation – which insist that specific peoples belong in specific places – help to justify uneven development and the immobilisation of the global poor (see Chapter 1). Restrictive citizenship and immigration regimes force the majority of the global poor to stay put, where they must accept lower wages (or no wages at all). When people do seek to move from the global South to the global North, they do so with restricted rights – as temporary, undocumented and illegalised labour. Borders therefore produce forms of labour market segmentation and racialised hyper-exploitation in the countries that receive and rely on migrant labour.[1] As Ruth Wilson Gilmore puts it, 'Capitalism requires inequality and racism enshrines it.'[2] Any account of how racism enshrines inequality must consider the role of borders in organising racial capitalism at different scales: local, national and global.

Immigration Controls and Work

On the morning of 4 July 2016, two weeks after the UK voted to leave the European Union, workers at the high street restaurant Byron Burgers were called in for what they were told was a health-and-safety meeting. Once in the backroom, they were accosted by Home Office Immigration Enforcement agents and asked for their papers. Thirty-five of them – from Brazil, Nepal, Egypt and Albania – were then arrested, many of them later deported.[3] Like Deliveroo and SOAS (University of London) before them, Byron Burgers went above and beyond to assist the Home Office in identifying, and in this case entrapping, their undocumented workers, when they were under no legal obligation to do so.[4] Under the 'hostile environment' policy, employers are deputised to act as border agents, and face potentially unlimited fines or up to five years in prison if they are found to be employing undocumented workers without having conducted valid 'right to work' checks (this does not amount to an obligation to facilitate surreptitious raids against one's own employees, however).

Enforcement of these employer sanctions is patchy, at best. But working illegally is itself a criminal offence for undocumented employees in the UK, punishable by up to fifty-one weeks in prison, a fine, or both. Meanwhile, migrant workers who are on 'shortage occupation lists', or sponsored by their employers, are tied by their visas, which means that if they lose their job they lose their status (as under temporary labour migration statuses in the United States and Canada). Meanwhile, overseas domestic workers have no right to change employer at all, and people seeking asylum are excluded from the regular labour market altogether. On top of this, many people on work visas have to pay significant sums, in addition to income and other taxes, in order to access essential services like the NHS, while also being excluded from welfare support through a provision which gives them 'no recourse to public funds'.

Anyone genuinely concerned about labour rights needs to understand that these kinds of border controls only strengthen the hands of bosses, making it easier for them to undermine terms and conditions for everyone. It is migrants' vulnerability to immigration control – especially deportation power – that makes them especially pliable and exploitable. The suggestion that migrant workers drive down wages – popular on the right and parts of the left – fails to account for the fact that immigration systems make workers less free and undermine their ability to assert their labour rights. If your right to remain in the country is dependent on you having a particular job, and if becoming 'illegal' means destitution and the threat of deportation, then it is very difficult to ask for a pay rise or call out unsafe labour practices. Similarly, if you have been pushed into the irregular labour market because you cannot survive on the meagre asylum support paid by the state (in the UK, £35 per week), or because you do not have the so-called 'right to work', then exposing exploitative practices, or calling the police, is not really an option when the police are likely to flag you to immigration enforcement. And so, the extent to which migrants do in fact drive down wages – however questionable this claim might be empirically – is an effect of their vulnerability to hyper-exploitation due to their precarious and sometimes 'illegal' immigration statuses.[5]

It is worth restating some fundamentals of left politics here: better working conditions come from the struggles of the working class. Despite the prevalence of common-sense claims that the value of wages is determined simply by supply and demand – so that migrant workers, by furnishing more supply, cause the value of wages to fall – it is in fact the capacity, or incapacity, to struggle collectively that determines the value of wages. When leftists accept ideas about 'supply and demand', they negate the potential and the force of worker agency and struggle. In short, better wages for all are dependent on the capacity for collective resistance; thus, building such capacity among all workers, including migrants, is critical. Immigration controls only weaken that capacity. Therefore, fighting for the rights and conditions of precarious migrant labourers can improve the lot of all working people. And the most effective way to do this is by building the power of migrant-inclusive trade unions.

Trade unions have often played host to virulent forms of racism; organised workers in both Britain and the United States were instrumental to the introduction of the first immigration controls, targeting Jewish and Chinese migrants respectively. But unions have also been central to anti-racist movements. In the UK, the Grunwick strike of 1976–78, which was led by South Asian women from East Africa, is rightly celebrated for the ways in which it 'brought people of different races and backgrounds together in support of the rights of migrant women workers, shattered stereotypes about Asian women in Britain, and changed the face of trade union-ism'.[6] Thousands of union members from around the country supported these strikes with mass pickets, even if the strikes ultimately failed.

Trade unions provide space and structure for the develop-ment and articulation of collective demands. In a racist society, these demands must necessarily confront racism. Indeed, unions are able to negotiate and collectively bargain around anti-racist issues at work. Educators, for example, can work within unions to get police out of schools, or to stop education data being used for immigration enforcement, or to refuse to comply with counter-terror legislation that demands the sur-veillance of mostly Muslim students. By organising to resist these practices in the workplace, trade unions can take a stand against the racist policies of employers and governments. More generally, trade unions constitute an important node in the broad anti-racist movement – supporting campaigns, organis-ing and attending protests, and helping amplify evidence of racialised inequalities.

Unfortunately, however, unions often fail in their mission to support their workers experiencing racism at work, as well as racism from within the union itself. The question of whether and how to support precarious and illegalised migrants has therefore been especially controversial. In the British context, some key figures in the labour movement have actively reproduced anti-migrant narratives. In 2016, McCluskey, then leader of the Britain's largest union, Unite, invoked the 'concerns of working people' to underline his support for ending free movement within the EU, claiming that 'workers have always done best when the labour supply is controlled and communities are stable'.[7] And yet, other large, mainstream unions – including Unison, RMT and others – have made significant efforts to provide better support to migrant workers and resist the 'hostile environment'. Indeed, there are many migrant workers organising within these established trade unions.

Nonetheless, migrant workers continue to be vastly under-represented in mainstream trade unions, largely because they tend to work in the least protected sectors – in temporary jobs that are poorly unionised and/or on zero-hours contracts. In the UK, it has been the smaller, independent unions – like United Voices of the World (UVW) and Independent Workers' Union of Great Britain (IWGB) – that have best represented migrants: a task that requires organising in particular workplaces and among particular groups of workers. For example, cleaners, security guards and catering staff in London universities successfully organised within IWGB to have their contracts brought in-house; many of these workers were migrants with precarious or temporary immigration statuses. IWGB has also been fighting alongside people working in the platform economy in their attempts to unionise – such as drivers for Uber and Deliveroo – thereby actively supporting and building power largely, though not exclusively, among precarious migrant workers. Meanwhile, UVW has organised with strippers and sex workers, some of whom are especially vulnerable to criminalisation, illegalisation and deportation.

Contests over the place of migrant workers within the labour movement have been just as intense in the United

States. Historically, the majority of labour unions within the American Federation of Labor were strongly anti-immigration, and in the first half of the twentieth century sought to extend the terms of the Chinese Exclusion Act to other migrant workers. By the 1960s and '70s, the United Farm Workers union was actively campaigning against 'illegal immigration' from Mexico, reporting strikebreaking 'illegal immigrants' to the Immigration and Naturalization Service.[8] And yet, at the very same time there was significant support from organised labour for the Civil Rights movement; 40,000 union members were mobilised for the March on Washington for Jobs and Freedom, for example.

Today, unions in the United States remain both sites of racism and migrant exclusion, and at the same time indispensable to the collective struggle against structural racism. To give one small example, while the United Brotherhood of Carpenters admitted to reporting undocumented workers routinely to Immigration and Customs Enforcement (ICE), other unions, such as the Painters' Union, have sought to defend migrants facing deportation, and have campaigned for the release of their members from detention.[9] Similarly, the Unite Here union has hosted trainings instructing members on how to effectively stonewall ICE agents, emphasising employees' right to refuse to answer questions or show identification.[10]

We should not imagine that workers are supported by unions from on high; rather, workers *are the unions*. Consequently, when unions expand and organise with and among migrants – especially those with precarious statuses – they are able to develop radical demands that will improve the rights and dignity of all workers and all migrants. With this in mind, there are some important non-reformist reforms that can be pursued in relation to immigration controls, work and trade unions. First, people should be able to access labour rights and protections regardless of their immigration status. States thus need to enforce labour-market standards, such as the minimum wage, in ways that are uncoupled from policing and immigration enforcement. In its 2009 'Iced Out' report, the AFL-CIO – the largest federation of unions in the United States – articulated exactly this priority.[11]

Second, all non-citizens should be able to unionise, wherever they work, and trade unions should therefore seek to include all workers, regardless of legal status. Unions should also seek to organise groups of precarious and especially deportable workers, such as sex workers, immigration detainees and farm workers. This would help build power among undocumented workers otherwise without rights, and help challenge the idea that 'illegal immigrants' and citizens are competitors for scarce resources. Third, we should campaign for an end to workplace employment checks, so that employers are no longer enlisted to perform border-policing functions. In the meantime, unions should pressure employers to refuse to comply with such checks. Fourth, we should seek to abolish all crimes of illegal working whereby non-citizens are criminalised for working without papers.

Finally, we should seek to resist and combat all immigration raids in places of work – and all immigration raids more broadly. By organising with and among non-citizens, it is possible for unions to create places of sanctuary from immigration enforcement at work, pressuring employers to refuse document checks, resisting the incursions of border enforcement, and supporting colleagues threatened with detention and deportation. Building vibrant union movements and growing the membership among precarious migrants offer a key means of resisting immigration controls. This can and should be done while emphasising that migrants deserve dignity not because they *work hard* or *contribute to the economy*, but simply because they are exploited people sharing interests with citizen workers.

In short, trade unions are sites of struggle, and we should be fighting for and within them – as so many migrant organisers already are. As prison abolitionists Dan Berger, Mariame Kaba and David Stein point out, trade unions are perhaps the model non-reformist reformers: 'Socialists do not fight for trade unions in order to institutionalise capitalist social relations or build an aristocracy of labor. They do so in order to create durable structures that undermine the power of employers to exploit workers.'[12] In this broad fight, trade unions must ally themselves with those seeking to abolish borders, which in practice means supporting migrant workers subject to immigration controls.

This priority has broad implications for left politics. Rather than pandering to imagined nativist constituencies – the 'traditional', 'white', or 'left-behind' working class – we need instead to focus our efforts on building new constituencies and power bases. Unions will be central here, which means we must expand our understanding of work and workers – to include migrants, domestic labourers and sex workers for example – while building power among the most exploited, especially those with precarious immigration statuses. That said, anti-capitalism is not reducible to industrial relations. The struggle against immigration control needs to be threaded into wider struggles for decent housing, healthcare, education and welfare benefits. Taking the issue of violent borders into the heart of local struggles, where it might not already be a central issue, is crucial in this process. It demands that the position of illegalised migrants should be made central to our struggles on all issues of social and economic justice. As Bridget Anderson notes, 'if we don't think about it at the start, then it will be introduced as a means of undermining organising and imagining new futures later on'.[13]

Border Abolition Is International in Scope

The anti-capitalism of border abolition is inherently internationalist. If abolition means changing all the relations that underpin the permanence of borders, then vast global inequalities, ongoing processes of dispossession and extraction, and the mirage of 'development' all need to be contested. Border abolition is therefore planetary in scope, and we should look beyond the nation-state as the default container for human communities. This is easier said than done, but it suggests the need to build connections and strategies with groups working in the global South – especially in the places from which migrants originate and through which they move.

People should be able to remain and flourish close to home, or to wander and travel, as and when they wish. Border abolition thus concerns not only the rights and dignity of migrants living in the global North, but also the plight of poor and oppressed people everywhere. This means the conditions that make people's lives unliveable where they are must be confronted directly. War, environmental degradation and the dispossession of people's land and livelihoods all compel migration; border abolition does not pretend that all migration is liberatory. But neither are we concerned with whether alleviating global inequalities will reduce global migration. People have always moved, and will always do so. Our project is not aimed at reducing movement, but at increasing freedom. Such a project can be sharply contrasted with the contemporary politics of development.

Contemporary development policies are defined by logics of surplus, scarcity and containment: too many people and not enough resources. The foundational assumptions underpinning development have changed; there is no longer any suggestion that countries in the global South will progress through several stages before eventually coming to resemble societies in the global North – nor even that the global poor will one day all be included in global markets. 'Development' is now a euphemism for surviving existing conditions, rather than making those conditions better. This explains all the present talk about 'resilience' (making do with what you have) and 'informal labour' (development without jobs). In fact, the dominant impulse among powerful states today is to use development policies to try to *contain* the global poor in places of scarcity. To give a key example, many African states now receive development funds on the condition that they comply with EU border control efforts. Since the so-called migration crisis of 2015, much of this support has been channelled through the EU Trust Fund for Africa (EUTF), which is designed to 'tackle the root causes of irregular migration'.

Some EUTF schemes provide loans and training to help people find work and set up businesses at home, targeting young people who are thought to be 'potential migrants', as well as those recently deported from Europe. Other schemes attempt to dissuade people from taking risky journeys – through campaigns, educational projects and awareness raising – although the effectiveness of these policies is highly questionable. The underlying premise that alleviating poverty will decrease migration is not borne out by the evidence – people who move are rarely the poorest, and tend to be risk-taking young people moving with the support of their families, or because they feel stuck (the desire for existential mobility precedes that for physical mobility). In these circumstances, providing people with small-business loans or propagandising about the perils of the journey are unlikely to deter them.[14]

Most troublingly, however, EUTF funds are channelled into various 'capacity-building' initiatives designed to modernise recipient states' ability to police, document and surveil people living in or moving through their territories. These schemes help strengthen police information systems, train police officers and border guards, modernise systems of national identification, improve border surveillance, and consolidate computer systems and databases in so-called 'source' and 'transit' countries of migration. In effect, 'tackling the root causes of irregular migration' means supporting African states to police, contain and immobilise unruly populations more effectively – all under the umbrella of development.

More broadly, European borders have been externalised, and prospective migrants are now apprehended long before they arrive on European shores, sometimes before they even leave home. Frontex polices the seas, working with the Libyan coastguard to prevent migrants departing from Africa, while the EU has signed agreements with Turkey to ensure the speedy return of irregular migrants. The immobilisation of the racialised global poor is not simply a national question, then, but a central preoccupation of foreign policy and diplomacy. Development policy is crucial in this project. The violence of this 'empire of borders' becomes obscured by the language of development, humanitarianism and care: We stop the boats to save lives.[15]

We must reject these 'humanitarian' conceits, and seek alternatives to development as bordering and containment. One non-reformist reform in this context would be to create and expand spaces and schemes for free movement. While free movement in the EU is broadly limited to European nationals, prioritising the movement of labour rather than of people, it is still worth defending and expanding. At the same time, if borders within Africa, Latin America and Asia were dismantled, creating vast spaces of free circulation within particular regions, then borders, walls and closed national identities might lose their hold over political imaginaries more broadly.[16]

A World in Common

It is no coincidence that the word mobility refers not only to movement but also to the common people, the working classes, the mob.

Dimitri Papadopoulos, Niamh Stephenson and Vasily Tsianos, *Escape Routes: Control and Subversion in the Twenty-First Century*

As many indigenous scholars and activists have stated: Land does not belong to us; we belong to the land. If no one owned land, there could be no nation-states, only commons – a world in common. Territory, on the other hand, belongs to the state. It is property. Citizenship, too, is a property relation:

citizens belong to the state and the state belongs to citizens. Border abolition recognises that the territorialisation of labour is a key tool of racial capitalism. As Andrea Smith argues in her foreword to Harsha Walia's book *Undoing Border Imperialism*, '[F]or immigration to be a problem, people must live in a propertied relationship to land. That is, [where] land is a commodity that can be owned and controlled by one group of people.'[17]

It is clear that anti-capitalist projects must seek to unmake sovereign territory. There can be no freedom within the confines of the nation-state, and the demand to abolish private property is necessarily a call to abolish the nation-state system itself – a call for border abolition. Ultimately, capitalism is a system that seeks to manage and control the uneven mobility of people and things. Anti-capitalism must therefore seek to provide people with greater means to exercise autonomous movement via the politics of border abolition. As William Walters reminds us, 'In certain respects the power of autonomous movement has been the hidden secret of the history of class struggle.'[18]

Anti-capitalists should remember that there can be no socialism in one country, and no progressive labour movement that puts 'natives' first. Because walled workers cannot unite, anti-capitalism is necessarily internationalist, which means committed to border abolition. Left-wing nativisms, on the other hand, offer only further means of justifying the immobilisation of the global poor, by which unknown foreigners suffer and die – but 'at home', where they belong. Migrant justice cannot be secured under capitalism. Capitalism relies on the constant reproduction of social differences and hierarchies, and trades on geographically uneven development. Global inequalities are therefore inherent to capitalism, and they are only getting worse. Thus, there can be no nice or fair way to manage migration; there is no way to make borders sufficiently 'liberal', or to put all the people in the right boxes.

Ultimately, border abolition and anti-capitalism are one and the same, and both must be global and internationalist.[19] To abolish capitalism, we must abolish borders – and vice versa. There is no other way.

4

Policing

Over the past six years, deportations of criminals are up 80 percent. And that's why we're going to keep focusing enforcement resources on actual threats to our security. Felons, not families. Criminals, not children. Gang members, not a mom who's working hard to provide for her kids. We'll prioritize, just like law enforcement does every day.

President Obama, November 2014

It's ridiculous that the British Government should have to go to such lengths to get rid of dangerous foreigners. That's why the next Conservative manifesto will promise to scrap the Human Rights Act . . . where there is no risk of serious and irreversible harm, we should deport foreign criminals first and hear their appeal later.

Theresa May, UK home secretary, October 2013

Darel moved from Jamaica to the UK when he was seven years old. He lived with his mother in West London, where he went to primary and secondary school, but he never regularised his immigration status. This became a problem when he turned eighteen and began looking for employment. Over the next few years, Darel had four children with his partner Shanice, all of whom were British citizens. Because he was excluded from the 'right to work', he acted as the primary carer for the children, taking them to school and preparing meals, while Shanice worked full-time.

Around his thirtieth birthday, Darel was informed that the Home Office was pursuing his deportation. Not only was he an 'overstayer' (an immigration offender), he was also accused of being a 'foreign criminal'. The assertion of his criminality was not based on any convictions, but on *suspected* criminality. Under an initiative called Operation Nexus, the immigration authorities and the police formulated a deportation case on the basis of police intelligence – including information on police stops, arrests and charges that did not stick, as well as their intelligence analysis of his 'criminal associations' – in other words, his friends and their social groups. Darel had not been convicted of any serious offences, but the authorities asserted that, on the 'balance of probabilities', he was likely a 'criminal'. Their argument hinged ultimately on the charge of suspected 'gang involvement'. Darel was deported in September 2016 – exiled from his partner, his children, his mother, and his only home in the world – all on the basis of what the Home Office called 'non-convictions'.[1]

Darel's deportation demonstrates the lengths that the British government will go to in order to enforce the deportation of those labelled 'foreign criminals'. Now, it seems, even those without criminal records can be deported as criminals. But the point here is not to uphold Darel's innocence – which would only leave the wider system of criminal punishment intact – but rather to identify how 'criminality' is used to justify violent bordering.

Consider another example from the UK. In 2020 the Home Office tried to deport twin brothers to two different Caribbean countries that neither of them had ever visited. The twenty-four-year-old twins were born and raised in London, which they had never left – but both received deportation letters when serving prison terms (the UK removed birthright citizenship in 1983, and so the twins faced deportation to the islands of their mother and father's birth – Grenada and Dominica, respectively). That same year, in the midst of the Windrush scandal, the Home Office was able to reintroduce deportation charter flights to Jamaica by asserting that everyone booked on the flight was a 'serious foreign criminal'. The Windrush scandal, which raised critical questions about the legality and legitimacy of the UK's deportation regime, was clearly not enough to stall the righteous banishment of so-called 'foreign criminals'.

These cases point to the ways in which 'criminals' are produced by and managed within the immigration system. Immigration violations – and even renting property to or employing undocumented migrants – are increasingly criminalised. Criminal convictions of ever-diminishing seriousness are now seen as justifying the deportation of long-settled people, many of whom arrived as infants (or in some cases were born in the deporting state).[2] 'Foreign criminals' – or 'criminal aliens', in the North American parlance – are beyond the pale, the ultimate 'baddies', 'ideal villains', and as such they raise challenging and urgent questions for migrants' rights advocates. They demand that we analyse connections between police, prisons and borders – between cages and walls – and that we avoid arguments based on innocence, victimhood, deservingness and contribution.[3] In short, the treatment of 'foreign criminals' points to the necessity of the abolition of police, prisons *and* borders.

The 'Foreign Criminal' and the Innocence Trap

> The ideal offender differs from the victim. He is, morally speaking, black against the white victim. He is a dangerous man coming from far away. He is a human being close to not being one.
>
> N. Christie, 'The Ideal Victim'

Historically, immigrants have been demonised on grounds of their supposed 'criminality'. In Victorian England, crime was blamed first on Irish immigrants ('dangerous classes' were labelled with the Irish-derived name of 'hooligan'), and then on Jews from Eastern Europe – whose 'criminality' was concocted from broader racist tropes about 'international Jewry'; supposed Jewish influence on government, banks and the press; and the alleged role of Jews in trafficking and prostitution in East London. These narratives prefaced the 'myth of black criminality' that has defined anti-black racism in postwar Britain,[4] as well as contemporary panics about so-called Muslim grooming gangs.

The immigrant has been constructed as 'criminal', and the 'criminal' has long been imagined in specifically racial terms. Whether referring to biology or culture, by measuring skulls or identifying cultural pathologies, the 'criminal' is constructed as an outsider, a foreigner and a stranger. These entangled histories of race, crime and migration – in which the racialised outsider, the criminal and the immigrant, often blur into one another – provide the backstory to recent policies targeting 'foreign criminals' and 'criminal aliens'. While 'foreign criminals' are enthusiastically detained and deported in various countries, this chapter focuses primarily on the UK context.

Since 2006, the British government has been prioritising the deportation of so-called 'foreign criminals'. In 2007, the UK Borders Act introduced the policy of 'automatic deportation', which meant the Home Office would automatically pursue the deportation of any non-citizen with a sentence of twelve months or longer.[5] Between 2006 and 2007, the number of 'foreign offenders' deported increased fivefold, and between 5,000 and 6,000 have been expelled annually since 2007.

Meanwhile, the immigration rules have made it harder for individuals to appeal against their deportations: the threshold for criminality has been lowered, while the right to 'private and family life' has been severely curtailed. The prison system has been reorganised around the 'problem of foreignness', with the introduction of 'foreign only' prisons, and the further embedding of immigration officers in prisons and police stations.[6] At the same time, people with prior convictions within immigration detention have the hardest time being granted bail, and therefore predominate among long-term detainees. In the exceptional context of the Covid-19 pandemic, 'foreign criminals' received little clemency; this group made up the majority of those who were kept in detention or forced onto deportation charter flights.

The immigrant who commits crime reaffirms racist common-sense, and 'foreign criminals' have long been central to

the justification of aggressive and punitive immigration policies more broadly – especially in relation to detention and
deportation. In other words, it is the spectre of the dangerous,
violent criminal 'foreigner' that justifies illegalisation, detention and deportation. This is why a politics of border abolition
should centre the migrants who are criminalised: because
narratives around crime and criminality play an oversized role
in justifying violent borders. Therefore, it is not possible to
wish away the stories and experiences of 'bad migrants'. In
fact, our politics and organising will be more consistent and
compelling if we recognise that borders and criminal punishment are connected forms of racist state violence. After all,
both criminals and migrants are denied the most fundamental rights of citizenship. And what is prison if not a form of
internal deportation?

Recognising these connections means bringing an end to
placards that read 'refugees are not criminals'. There has long
been a tendency within the liberal migrants' rights sector to
emphasise the specific vulnerabilities and remarkable talents
of 'genuine refugees', who are then implicitly (or explicitly)
contrasted with economic migrants and 'criminals'. Constructing refugees as innocent victims makes them eligible for
rights due to their suffering. However, emptying detention
centres of the innocent does very little to challenge their
fundamental logic. As Ruth Wilson Gilmore reminds us, the
challenge 'is not to figure out how to determine or prove the
innocence of certain individuals or certain classes of people,
but to attack the general system through which criminalisation proceeds'.[7] Campaigns for migrants' rights must contend
with thorny issues surrounding criminalised migrants, and
develop arguments that avoid binaries of innocence versus

guilt, victims versus villains, deserving versus undeserving. One approach would be to work out which kinds of argument hold for criminalised people, and to build out from there – or to evaluate particular campaigns in light of what they imply for those with criminal records.

In the British context, there are many issues we could fight for that would benefit 'foreign criminals' – and, by extension, *everyone* subject to immigration controls. We should campaign to end the policy of 'automatic deportation', removing the assumption that non-citizens in the criminal punishment system should be deported by default. Before 2007, criminalised non-citizens were often deported, but their cases were assessed on the basis of several factors: personal ties in the UK and the country of their citizenship, family life, the nature of the criminal conviction, age (upon arrival and upon conviction), as well as other relevant personal circumstances. The idea that there is an overwhelming 'public interest' in deporting any and every one with a criminal record had not yet been established, and so people who arrived in the UK as infants were mostly spared deportation. It is perfectly feasible that the UK could return to such a model, even while we also work to disrupt the notion that criminalisation is an effective way to respond to harm, and that deportation could ever be a just consequence.

More broadly, to improve the outcomes for criminalised migrants substantively, we need to increase access to justice for all migrants. In the UK, there have been sweeping cuts to legal aid in the last decade that have left many non-citizens unable to secure decent and affordable representation. If campaigners were able to secure greater access to legal aid and extend the scope of decent, free representation, this would significantly improve outcomes for individuals facing deportation. Relatedly, criminalised migrants are often deported despite their family ties. The right to respect for private and family life – enshrined in Article 8 of the European Convention on Human Rights – has been hollowed out. We should not only defend Article 8, but seek to expand the ways in which private and family life can be recognised and valued. Despite the attendant dangers of reproducing heteronormative family scripts, rights to family life do provide important lifelines for people facing deportation. By extending their remit we might be able to limit powers of deportation.

We should also campaign to end deportation charter flights (which are repeatedly justified by the putative criminality of those booked on them), and to end indefinite detention – in fact, to close detention centres altogether. This would reduce the carceral reach of the immigration regime, benefiting everyone facing the threat of deportation. We might also campaign to prevent the deportation of people who arrived in the country as infants, setting a cut-off point so that people who arrived before a certain age – or who have lived in the UK for a particular length of time – simply cannot be deported at all, regardless of the seriousness of any offence they might have committed, because they are de facto nationals.

None of these reforms are perfect, and all of them risk creating new divisions and lines of exclusion: What about those who arrived as adults? What about those who do not have children, partners or a family? What about those who have good lawyers and access to legal aid, but still lose their deportation cases? None of these reforms – however non-reformist – fundamentally overcome the violence of deportation. Still, they would significantly improve the prospects of thousands of people, and would together reduce the remit of the detention estate and the deportation regime. Crucially, they would benefit all migrants who face deportation, in a way in which policies for specific categories of vulnerable and deserving migrants – such as 'child refugees' and 'victims of trafficking' – do not. This is because they do not reproduce arguments about innocence, contribution and victimhood – which always infantilise and exclude – even if they do still rely on arguments about belonging.

Another issue deserving of the attention of campaigners relates to the criminalisation of immigration violations. Increasingly, states are creating new crimes of immigration. These include illegal entry or re-entry; overstaying a visa; working without papers; using fraudulent documents to access employment and public services; and assisting migrants to cross borders. Since 2016, people defined as 'illegal workers' in the UK can face six-month prison sentences with an unlimited fine if they are found working without the correct paperwork – and any income the individual earned from working illegally may be seized by the Home Office. More recently, the home secretary, Priti Patel, has vowed to close routes to asylum, and to introduce 'new maximum life sentences for people smugglers and facilitators'.[8] Meanwhile, in continental Europe, activists and humanitarians who assist and rescue stranded migrants in the Mediterranean Sea are facing lengthy prison sentences for smuggling offences, while in the United States tens of thousands are criminally prosecuted each year simply for illegal entry or re-entry to US territory. Moving and staying without authorisation are now criminal offences, subject to the full force of the criminal law.

This group of offences is what most people imagine when they think about the 'criminalisation of migration'. These policies are controversial, and evidently draconian, and perhaps therefore represent a weak point worth campaigning around. At the same time, many of these criminal laws are underused, prosecution being only a last resort. There is often more than enough latitude within immigration law to allow states to effect deportation without the need to resort to criminalisation. Indeed, the problem for many migrants is not one of criminalisation so much as the lack of criminal due process rights, and the inability to have one's case heard in any court in the first place.

More importantly, there is a danger that, in campaigning against the criminalisation of immigration, we might end up arguing that the individuals in question *are not really criminals* – echoing Barack Obama's instinctive contrasting of violent 'gangs' and 'felons' with 'working moms'. In short, even if we might wish to relegate immigration enforcement to the civil rather than the criminal arena for the time being, it is important not to isolate immigration crimes from other crimes. Here, we can turn to those working towards prison and police abolition, who must always contend with the ultimate question: What about the rapists and murderers? The answers they rehearse can help us defend criminalised non-citizens, whatever their offences.

Learning from Prison Abolition

When, as happens all too often, prison abolitionists are faced with the question: What about the rapists and murderers?, they reply by laying out some of the core tenets of abolitionist politics. They insist that we cannot usefully respond to violence by inflicting more violence, and that we therefore need to move beyond vengeance and punishment. They remind us that the criminal punishment system does not respond to or alleviate most forms of social harm. People die, are left to die, and are killed in multiple ways that are never defined as crimes or made subject to criminal law. Poverty, structural violence, slow death, social murder, corporate crime, death at work: none of these structural phenomena are what we have in mind when we discuss crime and criminals. Equally, gendered violence is endemic, and most acts of sexual violence and abuse will never be addressed in court. Locking up a handful of perpetrators – mostly the poor and racialised ones – does little to challenge gendered violence or improve safety.

Prison abolitionists do not shy away from the horrifying scale of this violence and social harm. Rather, they ask us who is served by locking away the poor and racialised people who are responsible for a fraction of it. Prisons do not alleviate social problems, they lock them away – and they do so by disappearing modestly educated people in the prime of their lives. Prison is a form of torture that does nothing to make us safer, and yet still most people find it impossible to think beyond.[9]

Prison abolitionists try to develop preventative and practically effective approaches to social harm – especially gendered and sexual violence – and have developed distinctive strategies and theories for community and transformative justice. People who enact harm and violence must face consequences – but accountability is not the same as punishment. Prison abolition rejects the binary distinction between victims and perpetrators, recognising that we all harm one another in various ways and are all capable of change.[10]

Prison abolition is not about simply demolishing prisons and keeping everything else the same, but rather about building a world where we do not rely on prisons and punishment because people have the things and the tools they need. As Mariame Kaba argues:

> Let's begin our abolitionist journey not with the question "What do we have now, and how can we make it better?" Instead, let's ask, "What can we imagine for ourselves and the world?" If we do that, then boundless possibilities of a more just world await us."

This emphasis on presence (the *presence* of things we need to flourish) rather than absence (the *absence* of prisons and police) suggests strategies for organising and campaigning. Ruth Wilson Gilmore's reflections on a successful campaign against prison expansion in California are telling here:

> [T]he California Prison Moratorium Project, which doesn't have the word 'abolition' in its mission statement, could join forces with grassroots environmental justice organizations in the Central Valley in order to fight against prison expansion. And to fight against prison expansion, we would, by joining forces, also have to fight on behalf of clean water and adequate schools, and against pesticide drift, toxic incinerators, all of that stuff. This raised anti-prison organizing in that region to a true abolitionist agenda, which is fighting for the right of people who

work in the Central Valley to have good health and
secure working conditions and not be subject to tox-
icity, in spite of the fact that so many of the workers
in the valley are not documented workers.[11]

By focusing on what people actually need in order to live better
and safer lives, campaigns against prisons can gain wide popular support. How might this be transposed to border abolition?
It demands that we convince people who imagine themselves to
be 'natives' – (mostly white) citizens – that borders do not protect or benefit them. It means fighting for better jobs, housing
and health without invoking a racist zero-sum game. To make
this work, it is important that citizens and migrants work
together, often at the local level, in pursuit of better conditions
for all. By doing so, the very categories of citizen and migrant
might be exploded altogether. Like prison abolition, these strategies require not only political commitment, but a political
imagination that prefigures the world we want to build.

Police and prison abolitionists also recognise that, to
respond to violence and conflict in our neighbourhoods without calling the police, we need to cultivate thick social
connections and practice local community responses. This
can be applied to community resistance to immigration raids
in homes and workplaces – which rely on building local networks of communication and resistance, ready to share
information, confront agents of the state, and support people
facing raids. This is precisely the strategy of anti-raids networks in London and across the UK.

Moreover, effective approaches to campaigning against
prison expansion can be applied to campaigns against detention centres. This often means working at a local or regional

level to convince local residents that a prison or detention centre should not be built in their area. Some of the most longstanding campaigns against detention centres in the UK have functioned locally. From campaigns against prisons, we can also see that successful strategies rely on multi-pronged approaches – sometimes being in the room with planners and politicians, sometimes protesting at the gates or supporting striking prisoners and detainees. Crucially, the fight for border abolition, like that for prison abolition, needs to be both practical and utopian: committed to radical action now while also to orienting ourselves to longer time-frames.

'Foreign criminals' are not an easy group to defend; to do so requires a combined critique of prisons and borders. With this in mind, we can see that the deportation of 'foreign criminals' is not only wrong because it is a form of 'double punishment', as is often argued, but because the *initial* criminal punishment was itself wrong and unjust. This is not only a question of unfair immigration consequences, but of unjust criminal punishment practices in the first instance. The important challenge is thus not only to learn from prison abolition, but to recognise that the policy changes we are fighting for are often one and the same.

This means that campaigns against prison expansion, and attempts to reform (or transform) drug policy through decriminalisation, are profoundly relevant to border abolition. Likewise, the decriminalisation of sex work would significantly improve the lives of many non-citizens (even as migrant sex workers must also escape the condition of deportability). As we noted in the introduction, the racist policing of 'gangs' leads to the deportation of young black men in particular;[12] thus, transforming society's approach to youth violence and drugs policy would help reduce the remit of detention and deportation in important ways. More broadly, the demand to defund the police – reducing their capacity, revenue and remit – and campaigns to remove police officers from schools are intimately connected to the struggle against internal borders. In the end, the struggle against criminalisation and illegalisation is always a shared fight; the cages and walls will rise or fall as one.

If the figure of the 'foreign criminal' justifies the worst excesses of border violence, then border abolition must be committed to their cause. There can be no effective campaign or strategy that reproduces the distinction between (innocent) migrants and (guilty) criminals. Criminalisation and illegalisation are connected forms of racist state violence, and the plight of 'foreign criminals' makes this especially clear.

In our struggles to dismantle borders, there is much we can learn from prison abolition. While we might campaign for non-reformist reforms now – perhaps engaging with politicians and large NGOs in pursuit of *less bad* policies – the success of border abolition ultimately hinges on the building of mass power and the cultivation of lived connections between citizens and migrants, both of whom are violated by the false promises of nationalism and capitalism.

Given the massive street mobilisations for Black Lives Matter in recent years, as well as mass protests against climate breakdown – especially among young people – it is clear that there are quite literally millions of people committed to transforming the world. The challenge is to connect border abolition to these lively debates on police, prisons, the environment and feminism. This is the only way we can win.

5

Counter-terror

We have made it very clear since 2011 that no British citizen should travel to Syria. Those who have stayed until the bitter end include some of the most devoted supporters of Daesh. One of the ways we can deal with the threat that they pose to the UK is to remove British citizenship from those holding another nationality. Since 2010, this power has been applied to about 150 people of a range of nationalities.

Home Secretary Sajid Javid, House of Commons debate on Shamima Begum, 11 March 2019

Shamima Begum was born in London in August 1999. Her mother and father were from Bangladesh but moved to the UK in 1980 and 1975, respectively. Both had secured indefinite leave to remain (permanent residence) before Begum was born, which made her a British citizen at birth. She was raised in Tower Hamlets, a borough in East London that has long been the principal area of settlement for Bangladeshis in the UK. Shamima Begum went to primary and secondary school in Bethnal Green, before departing for Syria in

February 2015 with two other school friends. They were subsequently dubbed the 'Bethnal Green Girls'. Shortly after
arriving in Syria, Begum married an ISIL fighter. She was
fifteen years old.

Her whereabouts were unknown until she was discovered
by the journalist Anthony Loyd in February 2019 in the
Al-Hawl camp, run by the Syrian Democratic Forces (SDF).
In that first interview with *The Times* journalist, she was nine
months pregnant, and she explained that she had already lost
two children in the previous four months: her eighteen-
month-old daughter and eight-month-old son, both of whom
died of sickness compounded by malnutrition while she was
inside ISIL-controlled enclaves. She told Loyd: 'After my two
kids died I just . . . Now I'm really overprotective of this baby,
I'm scared that this baby is going to get sick in this
camp . . . That's why I really want to get back to Britain,
because I know it will get taken care of, health-wise at least.'[1]
Three days later, Begum gave birth to her son, Jarrah. Three
days after that, the home secretary revoked her citizenship.
Two weeks later, on 7 March 2019, Jarrah died of pneumonia,
reportedly as a result of the dire conditions in the SDF-run
camps and a lack of effective medical treatment. Jarrah was a
British citizen.

Despite significant public support for Begum's exclusion,
expulsion and abandonment, fraught legal questions over her
nationality could not be so easily brushed over. Her claim to
Bangladeshi citizenship was tenuous – she had never lived
there, and the Bangladeshi government stated that she would
not be welcome there. She was thus vulnerable to statelessness, which raised critical questions over the home secretary's
power to denationalise her. Moreover, the fact that she left the

UK to join ISIL at fifteen led many to argue that she had been 'groomed', and that she should be returned to the UK on those grounds. But Begum's attempts to return to the UK to have her appeal against citizenship deprivation heard failed at the Supreme Court in February 2021. And so, at the time of writing, she remains in a refugee camp in Northern Syria.

The deprivation of Shamima Begum's citizenship forms part of a larger pattern in which the UK has significantly expanded its use of denationalisation in recent years, with the legal threshold for doing so creeping ever lower. In the context of the War on Terror, and attendant moral panics about Muslims and migrants, citizenship has come to be defined as a privilege – something to be earned, continually, and therefore something that can be removed.[2] The increased use of citizenship-stripping demonstrates the precarity and impermanence of citizenship rights for those defined as terrorists, enemies and serious criminals.[3] Importantly for our purposes, this means that immigration controls have been central to counter-terror policy and strategy. Minority citizens can be first turned into migrants, and then subjected to exclusion and deportation.

Just as importantly, the spectre of 'terrorism' is used to justify the punitive immigration restrictions that affect all migrants. Migration is repeatedly associated with terrorism and the civilisational threat of Islam, and debates about migration and borders thus become saturated by martial metaphors. Immigration becomes an invasion, a security threat, a state of emergency; enemies and outsiders must be detained, interned, denied access to legal rights, deported, banished. In short, contemporary borders have been shaped fundamentally by the War on Terror. A politics of border abolition needs to be firmly connected to struggles against counter-terror practices, the demonisation of Islam and Muslims, and the lethal impulse towards war more generally.

The War on Terror and the Abrogation of Citizenship

The War on Terror is an interminable kind of war – a global counterinsurgency against an everywhere enemy. The invasions of Afghanistan and Iraq – and the human catastrophes which followed and continue to unfold – heralded the global War on Terror, and the threat of global terrorism has justified torture, extraordinary rendition, the use of black sites, and various 'emergency measures' designed to identify and thwart 'terrorists'. More routinely, the threat of terrorism has made necessary the mandatory use of standardised passports and biometrics for travel across borders. As is well known, 9/11 and its aftershocks precipitated an intensification of bordering.[4]

Immigration controls have been central to counter-terrorism policy, providing states with the means to exclude, detain, and expel suspected terrorists. Immigrants have long been subject to legal exclusion, administrative detention without trial, and deportation – and so it is unsurprising that immigration controls have proved especially useful for states concerned with identifying and detaining suspected foreign terrorists. Importantly, though, 'terrorists' are often described as 'home-grown'– minority citizens nurtured in *our* local schools, neighbourhoods and religious institutions. Thus, we confront the problem of the internal enemy: national citizens turned Islamist combatants – or at least radicalised proto-terrorists. Citizenship-stripping has been central to the state response here, and the UK government has in many ways led the way.

Despite existing on the books for some time, citizenship deprivation powers were not used at all between 1973 and 2002 in Britain. The Nationality, Immigration and Asylum Act 2002 extended the state's powers of deprivation; where previously only naturalised citizens could be deprived, now even those born British could be denationalised if they had done anything 'seriously prejudicial to the vital interests of the UK'. The 2006 Act lowered the bar further, so that an individual could be deprived of citizenship if the secretary of state was satisfied that deprivation was 'conducive to the public good' (the same threshold as deportation). Both Acts included clauses preventing statelessness (required under international law), so that the powers only applied to dual nationals (whether naturalised or born British). In the Immigration Act 2014, however, the law was amended to allow deprivation where it might cause statelessness, if the secretary of state had 'reasonable grounds' for thinking the person would be able to acquire citizenship in another country. It was these powers that were used to deprive Shamima Begum of her citizenship.

It is estimated that hundreds of people have been deprived of their citizenship since 2010. Former home secretary Sajid Javid said that over 150 people had been stripped of their citizenship on the basis of terrorism and serious crime between 2010 and 2019. Britain is therefore an important case study in citizenship deprivation powers, not least because many other states have followed its lead – countries including Canada, Belgium, Australia, Germany, France, and Sweden. As Nisha Kapoor explains, 'While citizenship has always been a privilege, the growth of citizenship deprivation legislation reflects the extension of border control from policing immigrants to disciplining citizens, reifying and furthering systems of racial exclusion. It is a shift that has involved growing reliance on and subservience to executive power.'[5]

It is not necessary to chart the history of case law on citizenship deprivation here, but it is important to underline that each time these powers are extended, more people become vulnerable to denationalisation, thereby losing the right to have rights.[6] What this history shows is that the government legislates when it finds its powers curtailed by the courts – seeking to extend powers of citizenship deprivation even where it would render people stateless, for example. For successive authoritarian governments, human rights have been constructed as a hindrance to national security, and this is precisely the 'subservience to executive power' to which Kapoor alludes.

One particularly important case concerns deprivation of the citizenship of several naturalised Pakistani dual nationals who were convicted of sexual offences against young women and girls in the north of England. The case sparked a national scandal. The perpetrators were described as members of 'Pakistani Grooming Gangs', and the story became a lightning rod for far-right mobilisation and the further demonisation and terrorisation of Muslim communities. The harms committed by this group of men were heinous, but they paved the way for greater powers of citizenship deprivation. In this case, citizenship-stripping powers were used for the first time following a criminal conviction that did not contain a national security or terrorism element. Several of the perpetrators were deprived of their citizenship on the basis of 'serious organised crime', so that they could be deported after they had served their sentence.[7] This broadening of powers of denationalisation represents a significant precedent.

While successive laws have lowered the threshold for deprivation, it is still the case that many terrorist suspects cannot be easily denationalised. In cases where 'home-grown' terrorists have no claim to another nationality, passport removals and temporary exclusion orders provide one solution. Kapoor and Narkowicz describe this as 'deprivation by proxy'.[8] Through the removal and cancellation of their passports, British citizens are effectively deprived of their freedom of movement and rendered undocumented, while temporary exclusion orders prevent individuals from returning to the UK – one of the most fundamental rights of citizenship. Passport removals and temporary exclusion orders are examples of untrammelled executive power, pre-emptive in nature and lacking judicial oversight.

Terrorism cases are usually completely shrouded in secrecy. As human rights lawyer Gareth Peirce puts it, 'The most useful device of the executive is its ability to claim that secrecy is necessary for national security.'[9] Nowhere is this clearer than in the operation of the Special Immigration Appeals Commission (SIAC), which considers 'closed' material in immigration appeals containing matters of national security. As a result, the defendant cannot see the evidence against them. Once their lawyer has had sight of the closed material, they cannot take instructions from the person they are representing. Troublingly, SIAC has now established a precedent for the use of closed-court procedures and secret evidence, and some of these measures have now been applied in other UK courts.[10]

Prevent, Policing, and Rooting Out the Enemies

Clearly, the War on Terror has provided cover for the extension of state powers to exclude, denationalise, detain and deport. These deeply troubling patterns suggest that even fairly timid arguments in defence of liberal principles – separation of powers, due process rights, respect for fundamental civil liberties – now seem quite radical, in the context of perpetual war and everyday securitisation. These patterns also reaffirm the need to build connections between different struggles against state racism – against violent borders, punitive criminal justice, counter-terrorism, and war in general – and to build solidarity between groups variously racialised as internal outsiders: Muslims, migrants, overpoliced and criminalised young black people, and so on. The treatment of Muslim communities and those racialised as Muslim in the context of counter-terrorism mirrors the targeting of migrants in important ways, providing fertile ground for mutual solidarity. This is especially clear in the synergies between the UK's counter-radicalisation policy, Prevent, and the 'hostile environment' immigration policy.

Launched in 2006, Prevent has been a key part of the government's counter-terrorism strategy. It aims 'to stop people becoming terrorists or supporting terrorism', and forms part of the four Ps strategy: Prevent, Pursue, Protect and Prepare.[11] Prevent attempts to combat 'radicalisation' before people are enlisted into formal terrorist organisations, and therefore involves collecting intelligence about the beliefs and ideologies of people who are not involved in criminal activity – predominantly British Muslims. Initially, this information was gathered by schools, youth projects and religious and voluntary groups, either under pressure from the police or as a condition of the £140 million government funding attached to Prevent.[12] Many organisations and public bodies did not want to participate in the controversial programme, and so the government placed it on a statutory footing through the Counter-Terrorism and Security Act 2015. This meant that every local authority, educational institution and NHS trust now had a legal duty to 'have due regard to the need to prevent people from being drawn into terrorism'.[13]

In this new regime, everybody is compelled to look out for and report on signs of radicalisation. This has seen young school children reported to Prevent for inane comments, and has had a chilling effect on student politics. For example, signs of religiosity, critique of British imperialism or support for Palestine have led to reporting and surveillance. The government defined extremism in the Prevent strategy as 'vocal or active opposition to our fundamental values, including democracy, the rule of law, individual liberty and mutual respect and tolerance of different faiths and beliefs'.[14] Clearly, the vagueness of 'our fundamental values' offers wide scope for varied interpretation.

The 'hostile environment', on the other hand, involves denying undocumented migrants access to fundamental services, including healthcare, legal employment, housing, education, a driving licence and a bank account. Like Prevent, the policy deputises public officials and gatekeepers to enforce these punitive policies, in this instance checking immigration status to help root out 'illegal immigrants'. Everyone is checking and being checked – when they rent a house, go to the doctors, start a new job or attend lectures – and the Home

Office has sought to access the personal data collected by large public organisations and even charities. While Prevent and the 'hostile environment' are on different statutory footings, both demand that citizens surveil and report on those who do not properly belong in the nation. Both have had predictably racist outcomes, and yet both present opportunities for mass refusal. Anti-racists should continue to campaign against these policies, and encourage people to refuse to carry out such checks and reporting.

Given the political energy forming under the banner of abolition, it is important to re-emphasise the centrality of counter-terrorism in the broader landscape of state violence in Britain. Terrorism Acts have granted police forces the power to stop and search people indiscriminately. In 2009, over 100,000 searches were conducted under the Terrorism Act; none resulted in anyone being arrested for terrorism offences, although hundreds were arrested for other offences (these powers were ruled unlawful in 2010). Under the Prevention of Terrorism Act 2005, the government can enforce 'control orders', under which citizens and non-citizens suspected of terrorism offences can effectively be made subject to house arrest: denied access to a phone, the internet, employment, and the ability to associate or communicate with other individuals; compelled to stay at a specific address, compelled to surrender their passport, and to cooperate with surveillance, including electronic tagging. In short, the power of police and the scope of the carceral state have been intensified through counter-terrorism policies, and abolition in the UK must seek to dismantle these policies and practices.

In this fight, we need to make it clear that policing powers used against one group will soon be applied to others – in ways that have implications for all of us. While counter-terrorism policies might seem to protect us, in practice counter-terror policing involves the intensification of surveillance (especially digital surveillance) and the criminalisation of ideologies and sympathies (a kind of *pre-crime*). The apparent exigencies of the War on Terror legitimise the evasion of due process rights and criminalisation on the basis of suspicion. We should not be surprised, then, when the police promise to treat 'gang members' like terrorism suspects.[15] Meanwhile, in the context of immigration we have seen suspected gang members deported on the basis of 'non-convictions', mirroring the criminalisation of sympathies and associations that defines counter-terror policing.[16]

In all of these cases, we can observe a total disregard for due process and the protections of criminal law, in favour of unrestrained executive power to exclude, detain and deport. This means that people regularly lose their liberty on the basis of security intelligence – and without the scrutiny, for what it would be worth, of the judiciary. The racialisation of Muslims, migrants and black 'gang members' is central to the justification of these expansive powers, and these forms of racism against 'terrorists' and 'criminals' interact and fuel one another. They are united by discourses of internal threat and national decline, and they position 'decent, tax-paying citizens' as besieged – existing on a kind of war-footing with various internal enemies.

Abolition requires us to challenge narratives of innocence, and the 'terrorist' presents the biggest challenge to this principle. Many people who complain about the overpolicing of young black people might not see the immediate need to defend the rights of terror suspects. But the policing of both is intimately connected. Ultimately, a person's innocence – whether migrant, criminal or terrorist – is beside the point: we must limit if not abolish the state's power to deprive people of their liberty indiscriminately, and reduce its power to imprison, torture and to kill. Crucially, we need to recognise that the racialisation of Muslims – as potential terrorists, as a kind of civilisational threat, and as the principal enemy within – is central to the justification for excessive state violence and the extension of executive power in our times.

A focus on counter-terror policy also acts as a bridge from prison abolition (which refers mostly to citizens, however disenfranchised) to border abolition (which centres on those excluded from citizenship: 'migrants'). 'Terrorists' are the internal enemies par excellence – especially when they are transformed from citizens into migrants. This points to expulsion from citizenship as the central manoeuvre of the racist state in the context of the War on Terror. Where prison-abolitionist demands can sometimes equate to demands for a more socially democratic and less punitive state – for example, redirecting funding from police and prisons towards the welfare state – the defence of the rights of enemies (terrorists) and non-members (migrants) requires that we think more deeply about who counts as a member of the political community in the first place. In other words, because 'terrorists' and 'migrants' are made legally foreign, so that they can be expelled and disappeared, their treatment raises questions about the problem of exclusive citizenship regimes more broadly – a problem not always considered within prison-abolitionist campaigns and organising.

Debates about terrorism remind us that the production of racialised outsiders is rarely just a national story, but one which is intimately connected to war and the construction of racialised global threats emanating from abroad. In short, the figure of the 'terrorist' – who is turned into a foreigner so that they can be detained, deported or killed – reminds us that struggles against the punitive and carceral state cannot confine themselves to inequalities and injustices between differently racialised citizens. Abolition must also challenge how the line between inside and outside is drawn – legally, coercively, and through war. Indeed, thinking about counter-terror policy demands that we ask difficult questions about the relationship between abolition and citizenship.

Abolish Citizenship?

Al Berjawi was Lebanese born and London raised. He was first linked to Al Shabaab in 2006 and lost his UK citizenship in 2010. The first US attempt to kill him was via a drone strike in 2011; an attack in which he received serious injuries. He was finally assassinated by drone in January 2012, after a telephone call to congratulate his wife on giving birth.

Chris Woods, Bureau of Investigative Journalism, *All Party Parliamentary Group on Drones*, 15 May 2013

The hundreds who lost their lives off Lampedusa yesterday are Italian citizens as of today.

Prime Minister Enrico Letta, the day after over 360 migrants – primarily from Eritrea, Somalia and Ghana – drowned off the coast of the Italian island of Lampedusa (4 October 2013)

Bilal al-Berjawi was stripped of his British citizenship. Two years later, he was killed by a US drone strike. Or, perhaps instead: so that he could be killed by drone strike, al-Berjawi was stripped of his British citizenship. By the time he was assassinated, he was a foreign combatant killed by an ally in a global war – a quite unremarkable event. After all, killing foreigners is what war is all about. Two years later, over 360 'irregular migrants' travelling in a crowded fishing boat from Africa to Italy drowned in the Mediterranean Sea. In response, the drowned were granted honorary Italian citizenship. In death, they were gifted the passports that would have made their fatal journeys wholly unnecessary – a ghostly, empty and overdue form of political inclusion. Considered together, these stories provide important insights into contemporary citizenship regimes.

Citizenship is central to the legitimacy and authority of nation-states. Citizens are the included, the insiders, the members; the nation is a fraternity, a family and a people. States represent and protect the nation and its citizens – if necessary, by declaring emergency and waging war. This is why, when minority citizens (usually Muslims) adopt 'anti-national' positions, they can be stripped of membership and subjected to exclusion, expulsion and death. Citizenship is a privilege, and the enemies of the people have no legitimate right to it. This also explains why the drowned can be incorporated into the nation only posthumously. After all, the nation should not only wage war, but must demonstrate honour, morality and leadership. Granting citizenship to the drowned forms part of this act: those who were unwanted as mobile, vital human subjects are embraced in death as a sign of the nation's compassion and humanity.

When states remove citizenship – before extraditing, deporting or killing – one message they send out is that they would not kill or deport their own citizens. Only foreigners can be excluded, expelled, and assassinated; citizens are included and cared for. But states do in fact kill their own citizens, and let them die – and, while citizens cannot be deported, incarceration is a form of internal exile. In other words, the claim that only foreigners can be subjected to violence is contradicted by the situation of socially abandoned citizens: homeless people, incarcerated people, and poor people more generally.[17] As Nandita Sharma notes, '[T]he idea that making Migrants into citizens resolves the fact of subordination and exploitation assumes that citizens are neither oppressed nor exploited, thus reproducing the quintessential nationalist myth that the bonds of nationhood *transcend* class'.[18]

Citizens are not equal, and they are not protected by the state. Our aim, therefore, should not be to include more people in the citizenry, but to struggle against connected forms of organised violence that affect both citizens and non-citizens: borders, police, prisons, the military and surveillance. We need to challenge the right of states to demarcate membership through violence, and then subject non-citizens to indiscriminate violence and abandonment. This is an anti-war stance of the most radical kind – one that opposes not only militarism, conflict and mass killing, but also the nation-state as a mode of organising political communities. This is the anti-nationalism of the dreamers who can envisage human flourishing only in the absence of sovereign territories and bounded political communities.

When we argue that this or that state practice is unjust because its victims were citizens, we implicitly accept that non-citizens can justly be afforded no rights – including the right to demand accountability from the same states. By reaffirming the value of citizenship we retreat to a national frame of reference; our internationalism and dreams of planetary freedom are foreclosed when we seek inclusion only for citizens. If what we seek is global justice and historical repair through the abolition of borders, then the demand to turn more migrants into citizens is clearly insufficient. What about the colonial roots of our present world of highly unequal nation-states? What about the contemporary role of borders in upholding vast global inequalities?

Of course, many will contend that all politics requires some kind of bounded membership – a demos rather than a cosmos. We do not offer a blueprint for what comes after national citizenship. The crucial priority for us is to reject the false promises of citizenship. This is why, in the domestic context, we argue not for amnesties but for a raise in the baseline of rights and freedoms for all residents. This means reducing the legal and coercive power of the state to illegalise, raid, detain and deport – and it means ending border checks in healthcare, welfare and educational settings. These demands should be prioritised above demands to increase the pool of citizens.

We recognise that not having citizenship renders people 'illegal' and deportable, and for this reason citizenship might appear to be the solution. Indeed, for individuals themselves, acquiring citizenship usually does bring greater freedom and security – and much relief. But granting citizenship to more people does not challenge the exclusionary logic of immigration controls – it only shifts the goalposts. Incidents like the Windrush scandal and the denationalisation of people like

Shamima Begum remind us that the rights of citizenship can always be revoked.

Beyond demanding access to citizenship for particular individuals and groups with precarious statuses, border abolition considers the freedom of those yet to arrive. And so, while it remains true that some people are wrongly stripped of citizenship, and many others are denied citizenship in the country they call home, the wider point is that abandoning, excluding and expelling non-citizens is fundamentally unjust. Border abolition should not reinvest in the magical powers of citizenship, but seek instead to explode its core tenets. Just as the settler produces the native, the citizen produces the migrant: the illegal, detainable, and deportable migrant.[19] Ultimately, the abolition of borders would ensure the destruction of these deadly binaries.

6

Databases

The preceding chapters have shown that borders are not just about 'immigrants'; borders shape relations between all of us. Borders organise markets and populations, produce racial distinctions and hierarchies, and legislate heteronormativity. Borders also fuel and are fuelled by criminal punishment and counter-terrorism policies. Some readers will be familiar with the story we have told so far. What is often less understood are the specific connections between borders and technologies of identification, data capture and surveillance. We might recognise that controlling immigration relies on inspection, surveillance and biometrics. However, in light of the Home Office's aspirations to become 'digital by default' and the encroachment of private companies like Palantir into the heart of public services, there is in an urgent need for anti-racist and migrants' rights movements to develop their understanding of how emergent digital borders operate.

For us, border abolition is not technophobic per se – but it is concerned with dismantling immigration enforcement databases and algorithms that profile and predict risks, emphasising that these technological tools do not function in our collective interest. Like other technologies of power, data-management tools and architectures can be put to the purposes of surveillance, exclusion and expulsion – and once developed are rarely confined to their original targets. We must therefore challenge the state's use of new technologies for repressive ends, and confront at the deepest level the unquestioned authority of nation-states to know who we are, to fix us in law, to hold information centrally and asymmetrically, and to compel us to hand over personal data in return for (increasingly meagre) rights and protections. Indeed, by exploring the role of data processing in border regimes, we can learn more about the shape and power of the states that govern us.

Campaigning on technology and surveillance in the UK has long been dominated by professionalised NGOs working from a human-rights perspective. Rights to privacy and free expression have been emphasised at the expense of a critical analysis of the uneven impact of certain technologies on different groups of people, and a wider reckoning with the social harms produced, beyond breaches of data protection and privacy rights. Although this is now changing, there can be a tendency for organisations to focus narrowly on specific technologies and what they *might* do – thus pursuing an analysis of rights that has a view from nowhere, lacking any proper account of the dominant state and corporate logics into which new technologies are inserted. This and the following chapter therefore attempt to situate debates about new technology within a broader analysis of the logics of borders and their harms.

The Hostile Environment and Digital Borders

Following a 2010 Conservative manifesto commitment to 'reduce net migration to the tens of thousands', in 2012 Theresa May outlined plans to make the UK a 'very hostile environment for illegal immigrants' (following the Labour immigration minister, Liam Byrne, who in 2007 had also committed to a hostile environment involving outsourced border checks). The hostile environment involves denying migrants access to essential public services and private goods by embedding immigration checks and data-sharing between the arenas of health, policing, education, housing and banking, among others. The stated premise of the policy was to make life so difficult for undocumented people that they would simply leave the UK of their own accord – although in fact the policies have resulted in no significant change in voluntary departures, but instead a growing class of illegalised and rightless workers, and an entitlement-checking infrastructure that affects everyone.

The hostile environment is an attempt to outsource immigration control on the cheap, making use of information collected and/or held by the Department of Health, Department of Education, the Driver and Vehicle Licensing Agency, Department for Work and Pensions, CIFAS (a fraud-prevention agency), homelessness charities, and individual police forces – often without a person's knowledge or consent, or even that of the frontline worker collecting the data. It was an attempt to implement a vast but relatively unsophisticated data-matching architecture that would enable Home Office immigration enforcement to take action against undocumented migrants using data collected by trusted public services.

These policies and practices became the subject of fierce public debate in Spring 2018, when the Windrush scandal broke.[1] The scandal drew attention to the violence of the UK's draconian approach to controlling immigration. However, by focusing on the exclusion and destitution wrought by the hostile environment, and those wrongly caught up in it, we might miss the more mundane but no less dangerous data-management components of this policy, which have important implications for how a resolution to the scandal might be conceived.

On some accounts, the problem for the Windrush generation was the fact that they were *under-documented*. Much was made of the revelation that the landing cards of Windrush migrants had been lost or destroyed, for example. In the digital era, Windrush migrants were at the whim of misplaced documents and lost passports. Secure computer systems can overcome the problems of endless paper trails and lost documents, and so for some the resolution of the Windrush scandal was in fact the extension of digital borders.

The anti-immigration polemicist David Goodhart, for example, co-authored a report stating: 'The often elderly Caribbeans caught up in the Windrush scandal were victims of that process being mismanaged, not the process itself.'[2] The report called for a national identity card scheme to be implemented as part of a wider crackdown on irregular migration. In other words, the hostile environment, properly managed, would require a system of national identity cards for all citizens, which would be connected to digital databases – and this would in turn prevent the 'wrongful' targeting of rights-bearing groups like the 'Windrush migrants'. We see this insidious tech solutionism replicated in calls by EU citizens' rights groups for QR codes for EU migrants to ease entitlement checks. Such solutions betray a damaging lack of solidarity with migrants without such entitlements, and ignore the fact that we would all be better served by universal access to essential services, regardless of immigration status.

In other words, if we maintain that policies like the 'hostile environment' are bad because they target the wrong people, the solution is highly likely to be tougher and more efficient systems of identification and exclusion. Here we arrive at one of the important points where abolitionists and reformists necessarily diverge. For reformists, making the immigration system better at classifying and sorting, bestowing status on the deserving, and facilitating the swift removal of the undocumented can be a worthy end in itself – or, at the very least, the most we can hope for on the current political terrain. The reformist perspective on the Windrush scandal, for example, did little to trouble the assumption that some people can rightly be subjected to a hostile environment when they are, in fact, undocumented or 'illegal'.

For abolitionist campaigners, however, the testimonies of the Windrush generation were vital not only for underscoring the physical and psychological harm inflicted by the hostile environment, but also for opening up space for broader campaigns to end the hostile environment for everyone – especially given that governments can redraw the lines of regular immigration status with such apparent ease. Ostensible anti-racists and left nativists who concede that 'welfare support is first and foremost reserved for citizens' would do well to remember that citizenship is not a safe harbour.[3] Trying to fit more people into the 'citizen' box does little to challenge the exclusionary logic of immigration control.

Identification and the Modern State

The ability to identify individuals and survey/surveil populations is what makes a state modern. States make people 'legible' – as workers, taxpayers, conscripts, criminals and migrants – so that they can be governed, administered and controlled.[4] Early modern states sought to make people legible primarily so that they could be taxed and conscripted – but this did not necessarily require knowledge of each and every individual. As modern states developed, governments sought to identify individuals with certainty, so that each person could be distinguished from any other, and information on the population became standardised and stored centrally. Verification of individual identity was important for various forms of contract – in the leasing and sale of land, for example – and for policing imperatives: Is this person a repeat offender? Is this individual a former deserter? The standardisation of names, the use of signatures, and later the use of photographs and fingerprints all represented attempts to verify individual identities.[5]

In nineteenth-century Europe, states felt compelled to identify individuals more reliably because the societies they governed were increasingly mobile, industrialising and urban. In France, Alphonse Bertillon developed his system of anthropometry (body measurement) to verify the identity of individual criminals, especially repeat offenders, while Francis

Galton, the father of eugenics, made the case for fingerprint identification in Britain. Unsurprisingly given the centrality of racial thought to late Victorian science, it was also hoped that, by gathering biometric information on individuals, racial differences could be classified and understood more accurately. Identifying individuals and classifying them into fixed racial groupings worked (and still work) hand in hand. In the late nineteenth and early twentieth centuries, the policing imperative was rivalled only by nationalist demands to control the mobility of aliens and foreigners, especially in times of war – and the two converged in the policing of 'vagrants' and nomadic peoples. The passport, the identity document par excellence, has worked to nationalise populations and make people's movement subject to more effective oversight and administration.[6]

Many histories of modern statecraft have been rightly criticised for their Eurocentrism, and it is important to recognise that colonial settings were often the laboratory for new technologies of identification and surveillance. As Simone Browne has discussed at length, the slave pass can be understood as a form of documentation that prefigures the passport; several historians have shown that practices of fingerprinting were developed not in Victorian London, but in colonial India and South Africa.[7]

That said, systems of identification are not in themselves good or evil, and they can in some instances ensure greater access to health and social welfare (it is probably a good thing that people can be identified for the purposes of vaccination, and that health providers can retain individual medical records, for example). However, given that the main prerogative of modern states has been to control and exploit workers, territorialise and nationalise populations, and police unruly populations, processes of state identification have been centrally implicated in various forms of exclusion. Identification practices always grant *and* deny access; in order to manage, control and police, you need to be able to identify, verify and retain centralised information on people. The technologies of identification have changed over time, but we can observe consistent logics of differentiation, segregation and exclusion long before the dystopian world of facial recognition and interoperable digital databases. With these histories in mind, we are able to interrogate the logics that drive the innovation and marketing of technologies like facial recognition and vast data haystacks, rather than simply gesturing towards scary new technologies.

ID Cards and the Database State

By recognising that technologies of identification are central to modern statecraft, we can also better connect bordering practices to wider state practices. In the UK context, for example, the data-mining and matching architecture underpinning the hostile environment cannot be isolated from broader state practices of mass surveillance and data-harvesting. By the late noughties, catalysed by the post-9/11 assault on civil liberties and a broader crackdown on crime and disorder, the UK had implemented a DNA database, a domestic extremism database, gangs databases, counter-terror databases, bulk interception of communications data, and more. Interestingly, the Conservatives formed the 2010 coalition with the Liberal Democrats partly on the basis of a manifesto that promised to 'reverse the rise of the surveillance state', following a years-long attempt by the Labour government to introduce a nationwide ID scheme – a scheme that would have seen the personal data of every individual who applied for a British passport entered into a national database, with the possibility of being issued an ID card on a non-compulsory basis. The system was introduced for migrants in 2008 by Labour, and partially rolled out in some areas of the country in subsequent years. Predictably, biometric residence permits for migrants were the only aspect of the scheme to be retained when the Conservative–Lib Dem coalition came to power in 2010.

The question of national identity cards is interesting in the British context. Unlike on other civil liberties issues, the chorus of parliamentary opposition has historically included a Conservative aversion to the idea of compulsory national identification cards. Nationalistic tropes about Britons as freedom-loving people, in contrast with Germans and other Europeans, and in conjunction with arguments about cost and red tape, have long made national ID cards difficult to introduce. As a result, 'a Briton is more likely to be identified by a car than by a card'.[8]

However, what we see in the digital hostile environment are the foundations of an architecture that could be repurposed well beyond the requirements of immigration control. After all, entitlement checks require *everyone* to be checked, not only those perceived to be migrants. And the recent authoritarian response by the Conservative government to the pandemic – on both vaccine passports and policing powers more broadly – suggests that that parliamentary coalition against compulsory ID may well be fraying at the edges.

In September 2020, *The Times* reported on UK government plans to create online ID cards and digital identity systems. Under these plans, people would be 'assigned a unique digital identity to help them with such tasks as registering with a new GP'.[9] At the same time, the government is borrowing a tried and tested voter-suppression tactic, introducing legislation to mandate the showing of ID for voting in general elections.[10] Meanwhile, the Home Office presses on with its 'status checking programme', which aims to further automate and intensify entitlement checks and data-sharing on citizens and migrants for the purposes of immigration enforcement. Clearly, the debate about ID is not now and never was purely a debate about pieces of plastic, but rather about the character and scope of centralised government databases. A digital identity system would make it far easier for government institutions to access records across a whole host of different agencies, from health, tax, immigration and education records, linking previously siloed and purpose-limited datasets to build up an intimate picture of almost every aspect of our lives, and then to intervene in our lives, granting or denying us access to essential services on the basis of what it thinks it knows about us.

Just as the hostile environment ushered in increasing demands for compulsory ID, the Covid-19 pandemic has further intensified demands for internal checks and digital registration systems. The Tony Blair Institute, set up by the former British prime minister who tried and failed to introduce ID cards, has long lobbied for a compulsory ID system. As soon as the pandemic began, it started lobbying for vaccine passports under the explicit heading of 'mobility credentials'. Many people might find it convenient to download an app that verifies their vaccination status or antibody levels – just as they might prefer to have one national identity number for accessing government services; but these technologies enable new and more total forms of surveillance and exclusion. Under cover of 'protecting public health', states have accrued new powers with relative ease. Biosurveillance tools that claim to identify risk at the level of the individual, and can be easily repurposed once normalised, have been adopted, when what is really required is greater funding for public health infrastructure, enforcement against unsafe workplaces, and social and economic support for people who need to isolate.

When it comes to ID systems, there is much more at stake than being able to fill in tax records more quickly, or go to the pub during a pandemic. The slicker the entitlement check, the more refined the capacity to monitor and exclude. And we know from historical experience that the list of those who fall foul of government is rarely fixed for long, and has a habit of expanding. Rather than massively increasing state and corporate surveillance capacity in a bid to make ID checks easier, we should instead work against conditionality in access to essential goods and services in the first place. While in relation to Covid-19 this means prioritising public-health messaging, vaccine outreach and proper financial and social support for those required to isolate, in relation to hostile immigration policies the answer is quite simple: remove the hostile immigration policies. This is terrain on which reformists and abolitionists might find common ground. One need not be an abolitionist to agree that police, health services and education should be firewalled from immigration enforcement. At the very least, we can agree that the protection of public health, support for victims of serious crime and children's education should take priority over immigration enforcement.

There are several non-reformist reforms that can help stem the tide of digital borders, many of which aim to disrupt their logics as well as opposing their methods and modes of implementation. In the UK, campaign groups like Docs Not Cops, Unis Against Border Controls, and Against Borders for Children have campaigned against hostile environment immigration policies, and encouraged teachers and health professionals to resist and refuse complicity with immigration enforcement. In the United States, campaigns like No Tech for ICE, and the integration of undocumented people's rights into broader campaigns for workers' rights and universal healthcare, have countered the spread of borders into everyday life, challenging the idea that only citizens should qualify for basic rights and dignity, or that human misery should be a valid source of profit.

We need to challenge and reduce the power of the state to make access to essential goods and services conditional. New technologies will continue to increase dramatically the scale and speed at which the state can exclude. This is why migrant rights' advocates, people concerned with state racism, and progressives more broadly must become more digitally literate, building coalitions that can challenge the private corporations and governments constructing technological dystopias. We need to consider the safeguards that would ensure that new tech is meaningfully purpose-limited – or, if necessary, banned – as well as the firewalls that could be implemented between health, education, welfare support, and so on, and immigration enforcement and policing.

At the same time, we need to imagine how datasets might be deployed in the service of human flourishing in the broadest possible sense. Those solutions will need to be more inventive than suggesting that a more benevolent state should be in charge of public data, and will need to take into account the political economies of extraction and pollution underpinning digital infrastructure. We do not have all the answers to these vast questions, but it is important to start asking them.

Digital Identification and Managing the Global Poor

The UK is by no means alone in its expansion of digital borders. The EU is planning to introduce a 'single, overarching EU information system', which aims to help member-states 'to more effectively and efficiently locate and expel those who are irregularly present in the Schengen area, through the processing of more personal data, gathered from a greater number of people, for a broader set of purposes'.[11] The plan is to make EU databases interoperable, so that they function as a single entity, mirroring Home Office aspirations to build a unified 'biometric services gateway'.[12] The database under construction, the Common Identity Repository (CIR), will have a capacity of up to 300 million records containing biographic and biometric data, pooled from various existing EU databases. This runs counter to one of the key data-protection principles: that the original data should only be collected for a specific stated purpose. The CIR will facilitate identity checks and assist criminal investigations, and data 'will be subject to large-scale, automated cross-checking to try to detect the use of multiple identities by non-EU nationals, through the introduction of a system called the Multiple Identity Detector

(MID)'.[13] This data infrastructure, which in effect consolidates various databases at the supranational level for use by individual state authorities, will create a capacity for identification and surveillance that was until recently unthinkable. Like the hostile environment 'status checking programme', it will be easily extended to citizens.

It is not only in Europe that governments are experimenting with new forms of identification. Indeed, many of the key testing grounds for biometric national databases are in the global South – primarily in formerly colonised countries in Africa and Asia, where privacy and data protections are weaker, and the options for policy experimentation and profit-making therefore greater. In most cases, the principal justification for the introduction of national databases is framed in terms of inclusion rather than exclusion: financial inclusion, democratic inclusion, welfare inclusion. By verifying individual identities, governments and international organisations will be better able to provide them with access to services – especially financial services (banking, loans, aid); or so the argument goes. These initiatives draw on the UN sustainable development goal 16.9, which seeks to 'provide legal identity for all', defined as a fundamental human right. However, like earlier forms of state identification, these technologies grant means of both access and denial, while more accurate information on individuals offers tools for more extensive control and exclusion by states and international agencies.

Since 2013, the Kenyan government has sought to implement a form of mass registration that will gather biometric and biographic information on every person living in Kenya. Under the Huduma Namba initiative, each Kenyan citizen will be assigned a unique identifying number and then a national ID card, so that individuals can be verified against the national database. It is argued that this national identification system will combat fraud, modernise the democratic voting system, and guarantee better 'inclusion', although the scheme's tagline – 'a single source of truth' – sounds somewhat more ominous. Numerous concerns about the policy have been aired, and in early 2020 the Kenyan High Court ruled that the implementation of the National Integrated Identity Management System should not continue without further legislation to guarantee the security of data (especially of fingerprints and facial photographs), as well as measures to prevent the exclusion of certain groups (particularly the Nubian and Somali communities). Following the judgement, the government introduced measures that responded to these concerns; by October 2020, over 37 million Kenyans had registered, and the programme was moving to the next stage: card production.

In Jamaica, a similar process has been unfolding. Under the National Identification System (NIDS), citizens and residents in Jamaica will be given a unique lifelong identification number corresponding to biographic and biometric data that will be 'held securely' on a national database.[14] This identification system has not been designed with the exclusion of minorities and migrants in mind, but it is telling that the initiative has been funded largely by the Inter-American Development Bank. Jamaica's economic and social policies are largely shaped by international organisations and more powerful states – whether in relation to tourism, economic policy, or, as in this case, national identification. The United States, the UK and Canada remain concerned about drugs, weapons and phone-scams emanating out of Jamaica – all of which involve transnational networks and the transfer of illegally acquired funds. Modernising the ability of the Jamaican state to identify each individual and monitor their financial transactions therefore serves the policing imperatives of more powerful states.

The point here is that motivations for setting up biometric national databases vary in different places – but in countries in the global South they are seldom straightforward questions of national policy; they tend to concern demands from powerful states and institutions for greater surveillance and control over the movement of people, funds and illicit goods out of and into the underdeveloped world.

Nowhere is this clearer than in the EU's development programmes, which seek to restrict and control irregular migration from Africa and the Middle East. In Chapter 3, we briefly touched on the EU Trust Fund for Africa (EUTF), the EU programme that commits billions of euros each year to an attempt to 'tackle the root causes of irregular migration'. Crucially, many of the schemes within the programme involve building state capacity precisely through the modernisation of systems of state identification and surveillance. For example, in 2018 the EUTF provided €5 million to modernise and strengthen secure identity chains in Cape Verde and Guinea-Bissau, in the hope of more effectively combating irregular migration and trafficking. Several organisations have observed that these EU-funded technologies of identification and surveillance have been used by recipient governments to control their own populations, denying civil freedoms and squashing political opposition.[15]

While in the UK and Europe modern databases might self-evidently be designed to create hostile environments for suspect communities, in the global South they tend to be focused on preventing people departing in the first place – although this objective is usually masked by the language of development and inclusion. The UN sustainable development goal 16.9 – which aims to 'provide legal identity for all, including birth registration' – might ostensibly be designed to ensure the ability of everyone to make democratic claims and access justice, but in practice it serves those institutions that seek to control the unruly mobilities of the global poor.

Indeed, when the World Bank's Identification for Development (ID4D) programme promises 'to help countries realize the transformational potential of digital identification systems',[16] we are reminded that it is not only the UK Home Office that aspires to be digital by default, but in fact the very architects of 'international society'. When the UNHCR uses fingerprinting and iris-scanning to register refugees seeking assistance – demonstrating what Mark Latonero calls 'surveillance humanitarianism' – and when the UN's World Food Program partners with data-mining firm Palantir to help manage personal data on millions of food-aid recipients (for more on Palantir, see Chapter 7), we are reminded that these forms of biometric identification and data-capture seem to evade critical scrutiny altogether.[17] We need to evaluate these systems to increase our collective understanding of our digital present. We also need to understand the enormous resources poured into developing border technologies, so that we might mount an argument for those resources to be diverted to life-giving structures and practices that would in the long run make border technologies obsolete.

Identity Politics

[Y]ou are not one, you are multiple, and you are yourself. You are not lost because you are multiple. You are not broken apart because you are multiple.

Edouard Glissant

Across the political spectrum, people seem fixated on what they perceive to be the problems of 'identity politics' – a term that now circulates in popular discourse wholly untethered from its roots in the black feminist politics of the Combahee River Collective.[18] The Collective's use of 'identity politics' grew not out of a conceptual abstraction, but out of an affirmation of the inherent value of black women, and of their experience and analysis of organising against the interlocking oppressions of racism, sexism, capitalism and heteropatriarchy. Identity politics led them to be concerned 'with any situation that impinges upon the lives of women, Third World and working people'.[19] Their terrain was the struggle for socialism, for abortion rights, against sterilisation abuse, and for better healthcare – a far cry from the discourse of liberal representation with which 'identity politics' is so often associated today.

For those of us working to abolish borders, the 'identity politics' of the Combahee River Collective has much to offer our organising strategies. Returning to it can help us to challenge closed and parochial identities that prevent the formation of wider solidarities and collectives.

But we should also think carefully about the challenge posed by psychoanalytic, poststructural and postcolonial approaches, which in various ways unsettle dominant liberal notions of identity and the self. They help us to theorise identity otherwise, in terms of unfinished and undecided processes of identification. They remind us that the self is split and fractured, multiple and contingent – perhaps unknowable, even to itself.

Stuart Hall described identity as less a fixed state of being than a kind of story we tell ourselves so we can sleep at night.[20] And yet, if our cultural identities help us sleep at night, then it is practices of state identification that might keep us awake. While theories of identity have in some ways become more promiscuous, states have found new ways to fix us. While we celebrate open-ended processes of identification, states have been identifying us in new and more total ways.

Perhaps, then, the politics of border abolition require a rejection of the tenets of identity legally and technically, in the same ways that twentieth-century radical theory has culturally and existentially. The abolitionist vision is a world where I am not only me, but many things; I am undecided, and I should therefore not necessarily be knowable to, or capturable by, any central authority, when I am not even visible to myself. In this way, when Edouard Glissant urges us to embrace a radical openness to the Other, this might require us to dismantle the systems of state identification that force us to be radically fixed, singular rather than multiple.

In short, maybe we are expending too much energy talking about the wrong 'identity politics'. To build the world we want to live in, perhaps we need to pursue a radical cultural openness to the Other, celebrating promiscuous processes of identification against identity, while also resisting processes of state identification and identity-fixing. Can the radical openness of the self and of culture somehow be mobilised against the fixing, policing, surveilling power of states? Imagining how these struggles are connected and combining them in practice will surely turn out to be much more revolutionary than refining our quips and gripes about 'identity politics'.

7

Algorithms

We are Black and border guards hate us. Their computers hate us too.
Adissu, living without immigration status in Brussels, Belgium

If we want different or better or more just futures and worlds, it is important to notice what kind of knowledge networks are already predicting our futures.
Katherine McKittrick, *Dear Science and Other Stories*

Unlike many books on borders, we have intentionally devoted very little space in these pages to the border as a physical entity, or to spectacular sites of violence such as Ceuta and Melilla, the Mediterranean, the English Channel, and camps like those in Lesvos, Turkey, Arizona, or Manus and Nauru. This is partly because we are keen to avoid normalising the slow violence of exclusionary immigration controls by emphasising only the most extreme. But it is also because we believe that, by focusing too narrowly on the physicality of the militarised hard border – in emphasising fences, walls and camps – we miss something important. For us, describing borders as hardening – calling the EU a 'fortress', for example – only captures part of what borders do in the world.[1]

Borders are increasingly mobile, flexible, virtual and externalised. States surveil migrants from the skies, their unmanned aerial vehicles scanning the deserts and the seas, far from national borders. Algorithms make enforcement decisions – who to detain, who to deport – on the basis of vast amounts of data, traces of information on people and things harvested from social media accounts, financial transactions and innumerable government databases. These state practices are being tested, trialled and rolled out as we write. What are the possible futures for immigration control? How are they emerging in the present? And what modes of resistance will be needed against tools that are not yet consolidated?

As ever, thinking through what these technologies mean for migrants and borders leads us to consider the shape of the states that wield them, and new forms of algorithmic knowledge and control more broadly. In particular, the nexus between governments and private companies in this area demands renewed attention. Companies like Palantir, Amazon, and IBM stand to make lots of money out of 'high-tech' bordering. Authoritarian, anti-immigrant governments are proving ideal customers. These corporations must be a site of protest, intervention and action for those committed to dismantling borders in the twenty-first century.

ROBORDER and Drone Police

> *In this 21st century, we have challenges, and I think we can*
> *use 21st-century solutions instead of a 14th-century solution*
> *called the wall . . . Even if you put in a fence, 'bad guys' can*
> *use drones to carry drugs over that fence. So we have to be*
> *more flexible, more agile.*

Henry Cuellar, Democratic US Representative, Texas

As part of its Research and Innovation Programme, Horizon
2020, the EU is financing a project to develop drones that
will be piloted by artificial intelligence and will, it hopes,
autonomously patrol Europe's borders. The drones – including quadcopters, small planes, ground vehicles, submarines
and boats – will operate in swarms, identifying humans,
weapons and vehicles, and sharing information on 'targets'.
When the AI independently identifies people who may have
committed a crime, it will notify border police. 'The system
will be equipped with adaptable sensing and robotic technologies that can operate in a wide range of operational and
environmental settings', the ROBORDER website explains,
employing state-of-the-art developments in radar, thermal
and optical cameras, and radio-frequency sensors to determine threats along the border.[2] As ROBORDER's technical
manager explains, 'The main objective is to have as many
sensors in the field as possible to assist patrol personnel.'[3]

With ROBORDER's pilot schemes nearing completion,
campaigners have raised concerns about the future uses of
these technologies: their possible deployment for military
purposes and their sale to various states outside Europe. There
is also concern that these automated surveillance drones

might in the future be weaponised – enlisted not only to surveil migrants but to stop them. After all, there are already several weaponised drones on the market – flying robots armed with tasers, pepper spray, rubber bullets or live rounds, and missiles – and it has been noted that facial-recognition technologies might easily be added to the ROBORDER system at a later date.

These automated and semi-automated surveillance technologies are also being rolled out at border walls. In 2016 it was reported that the Turkish authorities were adding weapons to their smart border posts along the border with Syria, in which the AI would warn anyone within 300 metres of the border that they would be shot if they did not leave the area, before then opening fire if orders were ignored. As is often the case with press releases about new tools, the towers' capabilities were subsequently discussed in less lurid, but still alarming terms, described as being 'equipped with various types of surveillance paraphernalia and connected to equipment that will detect any sort of irregular movement across the green border'.[4]

Meanwhile, Saudi Arabia has built thousands of miles of border wall, both at the northern border with Iraq and the southern border with Yemen, employing watch towers with night-vision and radar cameras. In Israel, border walls are taken to new extremes and densities, with plans to build reinforced concrete walls underground to prevent tunnelling at the West Bank, Gaza, and the Northern borders with Lebanon and Syria. The Israeli state has long used smart technology, motion sensors and aerial surveillance at all its borders, and the southern border with Egypt has now been fortified with a 150-mile-long smart fence with observation towers, cameras, radar, motion detectors, barbed-wire and twenty-four-hour monitoring – primarily in response to concerns about 'illegal immigration'.

The US government offers perhaps the biggest market for border security tools, and for Customs and Border Protection (CBP) 'smart tech' is becoming increasingly important. Various Silicon Valley companies are pitching their AI drones to CBP, which has expressed interest in equipping drones with facial-recognition technology.[5] However, while drones may work well for targeted surveillance, they are not well suited to monitoring wide stretches of land over longer periods of time. The US government wants to implement a 'virtual' border wall, and companies like Anduril and Google are promising to deliver the tech solutions. Borders are increasingly intended to be invisible.

On its website, Anduril boasts of 'cutting-edge hardware and software products that solve complex national security challenges for America and its allies' (Peter Thiel, who set up Palantir, is one of the Anduril's key investors).[6] Like ROBOR-DER, the Anduril virtual wall system relies on autonomous helicopter drones operated in conjunction with sentry towers, using high-tech cameras, radar antennae, lasers and other sophisticated sensors to detect unauthorised entry. Anduril's AI software then processes all this data, automatically flagging suspicious-looking vehicles and people to border agencies. Google's Cloud technology will be used in tandem with Anduril's software, and it appears that Google's AI will be used to train the algorithm in object recognition, which will assist with detecting and categorising people and objects from images and video files. Despite protests from tech workers at Google over previous contracts with the Pentagon, it appears the company is now committed to servicing and profiting from the US border industry.

AI Border Agents, New Biometrics and Interoperable Databases

In 2018, the EU announced that it was piloting iBorderCtrl, a computerised lie-detection test for travellers seeking entry to Europe. According to the project coordinator, 'iBorderCtrl's system will collect data that will move beyond biometrics and on to biomarkers of deceit'.[7] Graciously, the animated AI border guard customises itself to the traveller's gender, ethnicity and language, to put applicants at ease as the software analyses thirty-eight of their facial micro-gestures to ascertain honesty and deceit:

> 'What is your surname?'
>> 'What is your citizenship and the purpose of your trip?'
>> 'If you open the suitcase and show me what is inside, will it confirm that your answers were true?'

The animated border agent asks these questions while, through your laptop camera, the AI scans your face and eye movements for apparent signs of lying. At the end of the interview, you are provided with a QR code that you must present when you arrive at the physical border (iBorderCtrl was piloted at airports in Hungary, Latvia and Greece). After a customary passport check, facial scan and fingerprinting, you may proceed if the AI thinks you are telling the truth (have a nice trip!). However, if the AI border guard judges that you have lied in your interview (what really *is* in your suitcase?), then your lie-detection score flags you as high risk, the human at the gate is notified, and you may be subject to further inspection and questioning.

Perhaps unsurprisingly, the technology does not work very well. The notion that you can measure whether a person is lying from facial micro-gestures is not borne out by the evidence. In any event, iBorderCtrl is just one example of experimentation with new biometrics at the border – new ways of measuring the body and attempting to establish the truth of identity and risk via biometric traces. The Canadian authorities have installed border-screening 'emotion-recognition' kiosks at airports, and the German authorities are experimenting with so-called 'voice-printing' technologies to determine where asylum-seekers *really* come from.

These new biometric technologies, which claim to measure voices, faces, emotions and intentions, are supposed to help states to screen, filter, and adjudicate more effectively, as they attempt to restrict irregular migration and identify security threats in an increasingly mobile world. In this way, they promise to make processes of identification, exclusion and expulsion more efficient and effective. In almost every case, it is questionable that the underlying quality these technologies claim to measure is indeed identifiable and measurable in the way that tech developers suggest. But for governments looking for a pretext upon which to identify and exclude, these fundamental questions are of little concern.

New biometric technologies have been most widely discussed in relation to facial recognition. Police forces in the UK have been especially enthusiastic about rolling out automatic facial recognition in public and quasi-public places – shopping centres, festivals, concerts, sports and community events, and political demonstrations – and have been collaborating with researchers on a live facial-recognition project that could identify people wearing masks or other face coverings.[8] Several campaign groups have focused on the issue of racial bias in facial-recognition technologies – pointing out that black people are more likely to be wrongly identified, for example. This might be true, but raises the obvious question: Would it be better if black people were more accurately identified? Complaints about racial bias seem likely to end in improvements to the tech, rather than the prevention of their use altogether. Further, it is not clear how effective arguments on racial bias are when it comes to new biometrics deployed at borders, or indeed in the context of war. Given that war and borders produce race and the racist world order, the concepts of bias and discrimination cannot do all the work we require of them.

This point is important, because biometrics are often trialled in sites of war and humanitarian disaster. As Privacy International reports, biometric data-collection in the name of 'countering terrorism' has been accelerating around the globe since 9/11, with little to no regulations or safeguards. The US military has constructed vast biometric databases in Iraq and Afghanistan, ostensibly to distinguish insurgents and terrorists from the local civilian population. Already by 2011, it was estimated that the US military had gathered the digital fingerprints, facial images and iris scans of roughly 1.5 million Afghans and 2.2 million Iraqis.[9] Today in Iraq, there are over 100 mobile biometric checkpoints, where over 1 million people have their fingerprints checked every day.[10]

Meanwhile, following the change of regime in Afghanistan in 2021, the Taliban seized US military biometrics devices.

While it was unclear how much biometric data was available to the Taliban, concerns emerged about the possibility that such devices would facilitate revenge attacks against those who had worked with US forces.[11] This case raises urgent questions about the limits of demands for procedural safeguards and purpose limitation as a response to the proliferation of surveillance technologies, rather than demanding outright bans. Without claiming that these systems are somehow more dangerous in the hands of the Taliban than the US military, this case reminds us that it is not always possible to defend against the ways in which systems might be used by different actors in the future – especially in the context of war.

Privacy International also discusses the Israeli state's use of cutting-edge facial-recognition technology, which in the name of counter-terrorism routinely surveils and severely restricts Palestinians' freedom of movement, as well as biometric initiatives by various international actors in Somalia that have had dubious benefits and detrimental effects on local populations.[12] The apparent consensus on the need to 'counter terrorism' makes it much easier for states and tech and defence companies to experiment with mass biometric databases, and to build surveillance infrastructure.

We know that biometric data must be stored, classified and made accessible, and therefore new biometric technologies cannot be understood in isolation from the massive interoperable databases we described in Chapter 6. The EU is now introducing the European Travel Information and Authorisation System, which pre-screens travellers from visa-exempt countries. Statewatch usefully reminds us that 'this data will not just be used to assess an individual's application, but to feed data mining and profiling algorithms'.[13] In other words, our data are not only used to identify us as individuals, but to train the algorithms that will decide the class of people to which we belong: who to let through and who to flag as high-risk in the future. Algorithms are thus about much more than identifying individuals more accurately.

Meanwhile, in the United States, the Department of Homeland Security (DHS) will soon require everyone applying for any visa or immigration status, as well as their citizen sponsors, to provide several forms of biometric data to the US government. The plan is to collect more types of biometric data on more people – fingerprints, iris scans, voice prints, and in some cases DNA samples – and to make searching and matching these biometric traces and profiles easier and more efficient. This forms part of the Homeland Advanced Recognition Technology framework, which is the newest iteration of DHS's automated biometric identification systems. Huge defence conglomerates have been the main beneficiaries of these contracts, including BAE and Northrup Grumman. Like much of the federal government's data infrastructure, this new biometric identification system will be hosted on Amazon Web Services. The development of this system is especially troubling, given that the DHS 'is known as a uniquely opaque and privacy-averse domestic law enforcement and surveillance apparatus'.[14]

That being said, we have to recognise that much of what we know about border technologies comes from sales pitches and press releases written by the people who hope to sell and use them. Within an overall logic of deterrence, these spectacular stories play an important role. Yet it is important to guard against assuming that these technologies function as their manufacturers intend them to – especially as it is in the interests of both buyers and sellers to conceal any failures and malfunctions. Indeed, we do the work of tech solutionists when we buy into and repeat stories of ruthlessly efficient, dystopian and all-seeing technologies. This is important because, in some circumstances, it can be politically strategically useful to demonstrate that technologies do not and cannot work as they claim to. Of course, there is a danger that the solution then becomes improvement of the technology itself. However, when campaigning for radically different policies, it can be useful to point out the empty promises and misguided imaginaries of the tech solutionists.

We need to be alive to the harms produced by the specific ways in which these tools do not work, as well as those produced when they do. If you are identified by a facial-recognition system as someone you are not, or marked out as lying by an AI border tool when you are telling the truth, this brings its own set of negative consequences, just as when the tool is 'correct'. While we might not want minoritised groups to be included more effectively in training datasets for these technologies, the harms of the tools not working also produce racist outcomes. Ultimately, of course, we do not want these technologies to work for these purposes for anyone. The point is that basing our arguments solely on whether technology works or not is rarely as effective as it can seem to be, and we need to proceed with nuance and care.

Profit and Prediction

The core mission of our company always was to make the West, especially America, the strongest in the world, the strongest it's ever been, for the sake of global peace and prosperity, and we feel like this year we really showed what that would mean.

Alex Karp, CEO of Palantir, January 2020

Immigration authorities around the world face one persistent challenge: how to identify and locate unwanted migrants. After all, 'illegal immigrants' are not easy to identify; they are our friends, colleagues, neighbours and classmates, and while they might be more likely to live in particular neighbourhoods or work in particular jobs, they do not lead segregated lives. For US Immigration and Customs Enforcement, this presents a problem: how to decide on 'targets' – which homes and establishments to raid.

Palantir's Integrated Case Management System offers the solution. It gathers vast amounts of data from state and federal law-enforcement agencies, various government databases (on visa and visitor entrants, for example), social media websites, utilities and banking data, both historical and live phone and text monitoring, commercial data surveillance and commercial licence-plate-reader data, providing access to over 5 billion data points for physically tracking individuals. Homeland Security Investigations then use this data to build profiles of individuals and their associations.

Meanwhile, ICE enforcement agents can access Palantir's FALCON analytical software on mobile devices, helping them identify targets for raids and build up profiles and intelligence reports, with real-time technical support from Palantir support staff embedded within ICE facilities in North Virginia. It was revealed in May 2019 that Palantir's Investigative Case Management (ICM) system was being used to track down over 400 family members of migrant children, while both FALCON and ICM were providing crucial infrastructure in support of intelligence, surveillance and raids. These systems rely on vast amounts of data that must be stored somewhere, and Amazon Web Services supports Palantir by running its software on the Amazon cloud service.[15]

The US government now spends more on border and immigration control than all other federal law enforcement agencies combined. Budgets rose from $350 million in 1980 to $1.2 billion in 1990 – then to $9.1 billion in 2003 and $23.7 billion in 2018. This astronomical growth in funding has supported an increasingly militarised border force, representing a huge expansion in the capacity to detain and deport, and – most relevant for our purposes here – the expansion of high-tech bordering tools, including cameras, aircraft, motion sensors, drones, video surveillance, biometrics and software tools for managing data and identifying enforcement targets. All of this has generated enormous profits for technology and security firms, private prison providers, and global arms companies.[16]

While the largest contractors remain well established defence companies – Raytheon, Lockheed Martin, Northrop Grumman, General Dynamics, Boeing – tech corporations providing digital platforms and analytics are becoming increasingly central to border and immigration enforcement: companies like IBM, Google, Amazon Cloud Services, Microsoft and Palantir. When a company like Palantir provides services to ICE, it equips them with the digital infrastructure to track, surveil and identify immigrants in new ways. Indeed, by identifying targets for immigration enforcement, these companies and their algorithms effectively wield sovereign power.[17]

Palantir gained its first contract with the US military using new tech to predict the location of IEDs in Afghanistan, before developing predictive policing technology as a contractor for the US in Iraq – technology that was subsequently used by police forces in the United States, primarily against the racial-ised poor.[18] Palantir now has tens of active contracts with the US federal government, worth at least $1.5 billion. During the Covid-19 pandemic, the company secured a contract with the UK's NHS, raising widespread concerns about access to confidential patient data and integration with systems of enti-tlement-checking and exclusion under the 'hostile environment' policy – especially given that Palantir also has a customs con-tract with the UK government. Palantir is especially controversial because its co-founder and key investor, Peter Thiel, is a far-right libertarian who supported Donald Trump, co-wrote a book called *The Diversity Myth*, and continues to invest in and associate with various white nationalists and the alt-right.

Given that companies like Palantir evince no shame, only pride, in their work for the security state, it seems unlikely that they will succumb to public pressure and campaigns – although state decision-makers, who are obliged to weigh a range of different public policy considerations, are more likely to do so. However, interrogating companies like Palantir, ana-lysing their software, contracts and political affiliations, at least makes visible the shady workings of new tech at the border. This can then open up a wider conversation about algorithms, predictive analytics and automated decision-making, helping to identify possible interventions for campaigners and tech workers.

This is important, because predictive analytics and algorithms are not the sole preserve of authoritarian right-wing governments. These tools are also employed by ostensibly liberal governments that want to 'manage migration' more effectively and make optimum decisions about who to grant access and rights. The Canadian authorities, for example, have been looking for artificial intelligence solutions that can assist immigration officials in deciding on humanitarian and compassionate applications, as well as pre-removal risk assessments – both of which are used as a last resort by immigrants seeking to remain in Canada and resist deportation.[19] Countries including Switzerland and the UK have been trialling algorithms to select refugees for resettlement. Similar computational tools are used by ICE to make decisions on who to detain, by police and corrections departments making decisions on criminal sentencing, parole and release in various countries, and by welfare authorities in countries like the Netherlands, which are concerned about benefit and tax fraud – all of which rely on processing huge amounts of data to produce risk profiles and predict outcomes. Algorithms promise solutions to problems surrounding irregular immigration, recidivism and 'welfare abuse', and governments seem only too willing to sign up for them.

It is important to note that the algorithms that make decisions about national security (who should be stopped at the airport and which container should be inspected?), immigration (who should be granted a visa and who should be detained?) and policing and prisons (where should we patrol and who should we parole?) have origins in less overtly coercive applications. Similar kinds of computation underlie the modelling that provides evidence on climate change, for example, or predicts the shape of proteins in the quest to learn more about cells, genes and infectious diseases. They are unlikely to be abandoned wholesale, and it is therefore vital to pursue the aim of limiting their permitted application.

Moreover, none of us stands outside these systems, even if individually we feel secure in our status as low-risk travellers, trusted borrowers or law-abiding citizens. We may feel insulated from coercive state power, but our data – innumerable traces of our lives harvested from online profiles, financial transactions, travel histories, associations and government databases – all feed and train the algorithms that go on to make decisions concerning the treatment of other people. In short, many algorithms are used not for identifying individuals, but for the prediction of risk, and the assignment of individuals to categories, in an uncertain and highly mobile world.[20]

This realisation should not lead to fatalistic resignation. Instead, the prevalence of algorithms and predictive analytics reminds us that anti-racists and migrants' rights activists need to respond to the digital character of contemporary statecraft. This became clear in the UK context when thousands of migrants on student visas were illegalised, detained and deported on the basis of a faulty voice-recognition algorithm that determined they had cheated on an English language test. Three years later, during the pandemic, thousands of eighteen-year-old school students joined together to protest their predicted A level grades, which reinforced and exacerbated racial and class-based disparities, holding signs that read 'Fuck the algorithm'. Around the same time, the Joint Council for the Welfare of Immigrants and the legal tech-rights group Foxglove won their legal case against the algorithm used to stream visa applications, which placed applicants in the 'red' high-risk group on the basis of seemingly little more than nationality (in response, the Home Office promised to redesign rather than abolish the visa-streaming tool, but this case represents a clear win in the struggle against algorithmic bordering).

To develop successful and astute campaigns and actions, we need first to build awareness and literacy in relation to digital borders. Too often, states and companies introduce systems in relative secrecy, with little public understanding or scrutiny. As part of the wider struggle against nativist and racist anti-immigration politics, we need to force governments to pause, to account for themselves, and to explain their digital systems and the contracts that govern their use. Demands for 'transparency' are both necessary and insufficient, but they do make it easier for us to understand what we are up against.

Where our movements are strong enough, potential strategies might include securing moratoria on the use of algorithmic decision-making tools and new biometric technologies like facial recognition.[21] This can secure us some breathing space while we work to defeat the broader logics of policing and borders that these technologies aim to enact, as well as time to build coalitions with people concerned by the way these tools might be put to other uses once refined at the border. As organisers in the US have made clear, this will have to give a central role to unionised tech workers themselves, who can exert real leverage.[22] Authoritarian governments and defence companies might be beyond the reach of public shame, indifferent to our demands, but the first step involves at least making our demands, loudly and clearly:

'Fuck the algorithm', 'Ban facial recognition', 'Shut down Palantir, IBM, Amazon, Google, Microsoft', 'Firewall the data' – and so on.

Algorithms Don't Deport People . . .

Contemporary bordering practices seek to restrict the mobility of unwanted people and things, while at the same time ensuring the speedy flow of other people and things. Borders are there to monitor, regulate and filter how people and goods move across them, not necessarily to stop or slow them down. In this context, 'security' means controlling circulation, not preventing it.[23] The world is supposed to be on the move, now more than ever; but the problem for states is their need to assert control over these mobilities, especially the sheer energy and restlessness that drives human movement. This makes technology especially important, because it offers the tools to observe, surveil, inspect, verify, fix individual identities, collect and process information, calculate risks and identify patterns.

You do not need a camp to immobilise and immiserate a person when you can identify them and strike out their right to have rights at the click of a button. Targeted bordering – which relies on gathering ever more information on people and things, harvested via more total forms of surveillance and identification technologies (biometrics) and processed by computational tools (algorithms) – allows states to exclude unwanted migrants earlier and more easily, while maintaining and facilitating the mobility of valued people, goods and services. It also reinforces a sense of conditionality and precariousness for those who, for the time being and for limited purposes, are currently able to cross borders, producing docile, obedient subjects. Borders are not only hardening, then – they are becoming more dense, more mobile, more virtual, and more pre-emptive.

Algorithms, computation and AI robot border-drones are an important part of this story. The developers of these technologies promise to replace humans – who are plagued by error, bias and limited brain power. In the process, they create new kinds of knowledge, truth and authority.[24] Algorithms process more data than any human could, and determine riskiness and worthiness through opaque calculations concerning innumerable data on people, things, transactions and complex associative links. Their complexity and novelty, and the vast amounts of data they deploy, lend them a veneer of legitimacy and scientific truth. Many are sold as helping us, and especially states, to see and process more; they promise to keep us safer in an insecure and highly mobile world.

But such new technologies do not represent a total break with previous systems, and we should avoid indulging fantasies of a 'robot takeover'. Human decision-making about who should go to prison, who should have their welfare benefits stopped, and who should be granted refugee status can be just as unfair, heartless and arbitrary as any algorithm. Indeed, it is through the use of reams of human data collection and decision-making that algorithms and the rules by which they operate are trained. Emphasising the lack of transparency and accountability in relation to algorithms therefore risks the acceptance of liberal fantasies surrounding human decision-making, as though rational, reasoning human subjects can reach fair decisions in courts of law, welfare offices and parole boards – as though the people making these decisions are somehow 'accountable' to those over whose lives they hold such terrible power. This has never been the case.

The problem with algorithmic decision-making is not simply that it is somehow less accountable and transparent, or that there is no human in the loop. The problem is the uses to which algorithms are put. After all, machine-learning algorithms can be used to predict earthquake aftershocks or identify cancerous tumours. Thus, the problem is not the technology per se, but the formulation of the problems to which algorithms offer solutions: the idea that movement across national borders is inherently dangerous and problematic, that welfare claimants are often undeserving 'cheats', that locking people up helps keep the rest of us safe. Dismal ideas about risk, security and scarcity – and the deeply sedimented hierarchies that determine who is defined a problem and whose life counts as valuable – drive the ways in which algorithms are deployed at borders.

If algorithms make new kinds of knowledge, truth and authority possible, the solution is not to make the algorithm less biased, to open its code up to scrutiny, or to put a human in the loop, but to challenge the logics of exclusion and expulsion that license their use at the border – though that is not to say that some of those procedural demands cannot buy us time.

In short, we cannot blame everything on the AI. The source of violent borders remains the uneven geographies of late capitalism, racialised global inequalities, violent nativism, restrictive ideas about gender and sexuality, punitive law-and-order policies, and militarism and war – all of which are articulated in new ways in the context of these emergent

technologies, driven by governmental enthusiasm for technological solutions and the profit motive of powerful tech and
defence companies.

~

INTERLUDE: FUTURES (1)

A Bordered Dystopia

Alberto lowers himself into the coffin. This is what he and the other drones call them, in what must once have been a wan attempt at humour. They are shipped across the dead ocean from site to site in coffins. He heaves gently. The anti-emetic hasn't kicked in yet. The cheap box is cushioned with a reddish mulch that will protect his body during the passage, which can be rough, especially if they're boarded by Frontex, who are known for culling undeclared Freight, or at least inflicting intentional damage.

The company insists that the mulch – also known as Infusion™ – 'provides 100% nutrition, hydration, and infection control through the skin barrier for journeys of up to three weeks'. That's some generous spin, of course. A third of drones die – fail, in company-speak – during the passage. The rest emerge weak and delirious, their muscles wasted from paltry oxygen rations; skin irritated from lying in their own filth. It's only with stims that they are able to work in the weeks that follow.

There are no words in the company lexicon for what the passage does to their minds: they are drones, after all.

The only rank lower than Freight is Waste, and Alberto has been relegated to Freight ever since he was put under 360. He'll probably fail before he comes up for reassignment. The pin in his fingertip begins to pulse blue as the sedative line activates. He will awaken in the same grim coffin.

Freight is moved from facility to facility as the company requires. He suspects the facilities are underground, but there's no way to tell. It's just a hunch he has because they're always warm, and he knows the company wouldn't waste heating on drones. Alberto doesn't know where he has been these last few months, and he doesn't know where he is going. Each facility is self-contained, and Freight does the same work wherever it's deployed. The facilities have no exterior of which Alberto is aware, and 360s aren't allowed outside anyway.

Alberto knows that this is an ocean passage because the coffins in the hangar unspool in rows. For land journeys, they are tessellated: something to do with the air supply. Humming dread washes over him, as it always does in the face of that indigo spoiled water. As Alberto submits to his dim terror, images of his Calculation swim, unwanted, into view.

He can no longer say when it happened. Freight rarely sees the sky, and has no way of marking time: the lights in the gunmetal facilities stay bright and blanking.

This – the Calculation – has brought what were once known as prison and work to an interminable convergence.

Flashing up on a glass screen beside Alberto's bed: Guilty, Freight, 360. Guilty, Freight, 360, a mantra: his designation and his destiny; the class of profiles to which he had always belonged, not helped by the fact that his childhood unit had also been relegated, for a perceived infraction of which his breeders never spoke.

By accident or design, there are no mirrored surfaces in the facility by which one might trace the ebb of time: the insistent greying or recession of a hairline; the track of new furrows on a cheek. Sedatives, stims and exo-suits are integral to the existence of every drone at the company. It's the only way they can be made physically and mentally to bear the repetition and relentless interiority of company life. For 360s, the unstinting use of all three blanks out any linear sense of physical demise or degradation of spirit. Only in the transitions between one phase and another – waking to sedation, and vice versa – does the pain of self-awareness pierce the cloud; but only for moments.

Calculation is how most things in company life – in life – are determined: the clean and final operation of an opaque set of rules on a body of data amassed by your surveillance feeds and, some suspect, those of your breeders and theirs, stretching back across generations. Alberto's Calculation was the result of his attendance at an unauthorised meeting which, unsurprisingly, was also attended by a mole.

He doesn't know where he is going, but he can't see why the company would bother shipping the 360s to anywhere other than a company facility. There was no need for the old way, of segregated prisons, when 360 was just drone life without company malfunctions. Drone or 360, everyone's exosuits were fitted with a slick range of monitors. But once a

Calculation put you on 360, no more random sampling – your surveillance feeds went straight to corphead. The ankle geotrackers actually worked. Rather than some vague threat easily evaded with the right tools, the collars would buzz you every time you entered unauthorised space. For 360s, that was everywhere except the facility and the sedation bay.

Even before Alberto's 360, outside was the preserve of those who could afford personal environmental regulation – either suits or adapted SUVs. Everyone else took their chances with the radiation forecast every few months, and used whatever junk they could find as protection from the caustic rain. He has heard myths of whole regulated towns and conurbations where the air is cool and the sky is made of glass. If they exist, they're North somewhere.

And so, as the sedatives win and he slips under, one last memory loop unwinds: goodbye to his unit, whom he remembers with the ghost of a fondness of which he is no longer capable; goodbye to the corrugated-iron trailer that he shared with his match and brood on the edge of quadrant three; goodbye to the weekly hour's rest and the freedom to spend some moments un-stimmed and un-suited, every once in a while. But this is some biological camber of his mind towards schmaltz: there had never been anything so crisp and clean as a goodbye, only a subterranean fog of frosted rage and regret in the liminal space of every sedation. Because when the Calculation came in all that time ago, it had at the same time activated his forgetting line, and the pin in his finger had begun to pulse green before he had more than an icewater blossoming moment to feel the loss of the little that had been his shatter through his gut and his legs.

8

Abolition

The future Alberto exists in is uncomfortably familiar, with its totalising convergence of life and work, and the use of opaque corporate algorithms to profile and punish perceived infractions. It is a future in which automation is ubiquitous, in the service of wringing profit from every disposable worker. In Alberto's world, the death-making movement of rightless labour is explicitly sponsored by the Company – a kind of indenture that works differently from the contemporary politics surrounding 'clandestine' and 'illegal' migration. This is also a world of minute, heteropatriarchal regulations of familial, sexual and recreational norms. All democratic possibilities have been foreclosed, not least those of organised labour, while the seas and the skies have been poisoned.

For Alberto, unfreedom looks like captivity – as it must, as we have shown. Alberto is a drone, kept alive to work in a world without light, only mulch, sedatives and anti-emetics. Totally surveilled, his life determined by the Calculation, he is denied even the limited autonomy of self: his memory, his reflection, his voice. Note, Alberto's world is not defined by border fences and walls, or even by nations and racism. Our future dystopian fantasies led us elsewhere, to a place where romantic ideologies of national community, belonging and shared destiny have become less important to systems of control and domination. There will surely be much communitarian violence along the way – racism, nativism, ethnic violence – as scarcity takes hold, the seas rise and the groundwaters deplete, while well-resourced people, territories and social classes are able to barricade themselves against the global majority. But despite the inevitability of new articulations of racism and nationalism, we wanted to emphasise here the centrality of technology to the forging of future dystopian worlds.

We emphasise this because traditional accounts of, and strategies for undermining, coercive state practices are failing to account adequately for the impact of new technologies, both in relation to borders and more broadly. Thinking centrally about the role of new technologies at the border led us to the nightmare of Alberto's world, a future in which unfreedom is made total by technology.

But the future in which Alberto exists is not inevitable – far from it; and we sketch it not to demoralise, but to illuminate what is at stake. As we set out in this book's introduction, for us abolition is a transformative political philosophy, an organising tradition that can help us chart a course out of our unfolding end-times. In this chapter we discuss what the politics of border abolition might look like in the present.

The richest seam of abolitionist work to date has focused primarily on what is known as the prison-industrial complex – the set of institutions and social relations that establishes caging, surveillance and punishment as the primary responses to an ever-increasing set of social problems. For prison abolitionists, the problem is not only prisons as physical sites of confinement, but all the social relations that make prisons appear necessary and permanent: the organised abandonment of working-class communities; the social force of racist resentment and hatred; and dominant ideas about security, punishment and war – where imperialism and militarism work alongside various wars at home: the wars on drugs, on poverty, on the racialised poor. Mariame Kaba writes that '[p]rison-industrial complex abolition is a political vision, a structural analysis of oppression, and a practical organizing strategy'; this book has sought to transpose this framework to the domain of border abolition.[1]

The abolition of borders requires that we challenge all the social structures underpinning their permanence. This means transforming the wider set of social and international relations that converge around bordering, as well as ending and dismantling the most visible manifestations of borders: towering walls, detention centres, mass deportation flights. Crucially, border abolition must take account of the phenomena to which borders are seen as a necessary response. Where those phenomena genuinely cause people harm, we need to figure out how we might transform the conditions that produce those harms. This is where abolition offers such a generative framework.

So, when we hear about how border controls keep communities safe from people who are convicted of crimes, we should indeed condemn the racist emphasis on 'foreign offenders', but we also need to develop ways to respond to harm, such as interpersonal violence, that do not rely on locking up and deporting aggressors. When we hear claims about migrants undercutting wages and putting pressure on public services, we need to build the power of migrant-inclusive labour unions and argue for greater social provision for all, regardless of whether these claims are empirically true. And when we hear about the harm to which migrants themselves are subject when they move – false imprisonment, sexual violence, labour exploitation, and so on – we need to end the forms of visa dependency and enforced illegality that produce these vulnerabilities in the first place. Abolishing borders also entails figuring out how we might relate to distant others on an equitable basis, wherever they are in the world, undoing the harm wrought by resource-extraction, environmental degradation and tied aid, and working to make the nation-state redundant as a political formation.

Non-Reformist Reforms

Central to abolitionist work is the identification of non-reformist reforms. Non-reformist reforms are 'those measures that reduce the power of an oppressive system while illuminating the system's inability to solve the crises it creates'.[2] The term was coined by André Gorz in 1967, in his reflections on anti-capitalist politics more broadly, and has been picked up by various groups struggling against capitalism, environmental destruction and, most notably, police and prisons.[3] While police, prisons and borders will not be abolished in a day, non-reformist reforms are those reforms that can help reduce their power in the meantime, while also making further progressive changes more likely in the future. Non-reformist reforms are those material changes that further open the way to a world without borders. In the words of Critical Resistance: 'Our goal is not to improve the system; it is to shrink the system into non-existence'.[4]

Non-reformist reforms can be contrasted with the liberal politics of reformism. Reformist reforms are those tweaks that make some kind of change while ultimately maintaining, or even expanding, the oppressive structures they seek to improve. Reforms that claim to blunt the oppressions of the border regime may in fact extend its reach: training and new technology for immigration enforcement officers; expanded use of electronic tags for immigration detainees on bail; replacement of human decision-makers with AI. The problem with reformism presents itself when our energies, resources and time are expended fighting for changes that ultimately move us no closer to the world we want to see, and in many instances might actively block our path. For those who can be contented with nicer, more liberal immigration regimes, such reformist reforms might suffice. But for those of us for whom abolition is a long-term goal, the task of distinguishing reformist from non-reformist reforms is a vital one.

We hope that border abolition can help to bring a wider set of relations into the frame – not just immigration vans, detention centres, Frontex, ICE or deportation charter flights, but also work and family relations, as well as the uses of emergent technologies of surveillance and data-capture in contemporary border regimes. Abolition helps break open the dichotomy that contrasts reform with revolution, and helps us think about which kinds of non-reformist reforms to pursue now. Moreover, because prison abolition emerges from traditions of black feminism, it suggests ways to centre racism and gendered violence that are just as productive for the critique of borders.

Abolitionist organisers working to dismantle the prison-industrial complex – Critical Resistance and Mariame Kaba, in particular – have helpfully set out questions we can ask ourselves when trying to distinguish between reformist reforms and non-reformist reforms in relation to borders.[5] What follows is our attempt to map a similar set of questions that apply in the context of border abolition. Our aim is not to offer a prescriptive, exhaustive list of policy changes we think should be enacted in the here and now. The line between reformist and non-reformist reforms can be fine, highly context-specific, and dependent on modes of implementation. However, if, in considering a particular reform, the answer to the questions below is 'yes', the odds are that it will be a more fruitful avenue for abolitionist organisers than one to which the answer is 'no'.

Five Questions to Ask About Immigration Reforms

1. Does it challenge the notion that regular immigration or citizenship status is the only legitimate way to have rights?

NO – Reformist: Immediate amnesty for all undocumented migrants; reinstatement of birthright citizenship.

Amnesties – that is, the en masse regularisation of undocumented people within a particular jurisdiction – recur repeatedly as a demand in countries with restrictive immigration systems.

We do not believe that there is a hard-and-fast rule that says amnesties are always reformist, but it is a significant risk in our view. Consider that, as mayor of London, Boris Johnson, now UK prime minister, backed an amnesty for undocumented migrants, while at the same time amnesties are a key demand of the #StatusNow campaign in the UK, and of the Gilets Noirs in France.

It is true that campaigns for regularisation reduce the reach of the immigration system into people's lives, as well as potentially breaking with the notion that migrants harm the citizen population. But amnesties also facilitate the absorption of a class of people into the protective citizen–state relationship, and are often one-time events that are coupled with a tightening of immigration controls against the remaining non-citizen population once they have been implemented. For example, Ronald Reagan's 1986 Immigration Reform and Control Act, which legalised most undocumented migrants who had arrived before 1982, was primarily billed as a crackdown on 'illegal immigration', promising tighter security at the Mexican border. Meanwhile, amnesties in countries like Italy and Spain have been temporary and revocable, directed more towards the need to gather tax revenue and regulate the economy than towards a more fundamental reckoning with the system of migrant exclusion and illegalisation.

Amnesties may also have conditions attached to them that prevent all undocumented people from being regularised: the requirement to have been in the country for a particular length of time, for example, or to not have a criminal record.

Thus, while amnesties might provide material relief to one group of undocumented people, unless they occur within a broader context of abolitionist reforms to an immigration system, they do nothing to ease the lives of people who become undocumented in the future, or to break with the idea that being a citizen is the only way to live a dignified life.

Likewise, campaigns to facilitate access to citizenship, whether by reducing fees for citizenship applications or reinstating access to birthright citizenship, reinscribe a similar logic, whereby a person must have regular status or citizenship in order to be recognised as a rights-holder in the eyes of the state. Like amnesties, this brings welcome material relief to some people and reduces the reach of the immigration system into their lives. But this does nothing to recuperate the status of the undocumented person or non-citizen as a person worthy of rights and dignity, and ultimately reinforces the logic of bordered nation-states as the default political guarantors of belonging. As Dimitris Papadopoulos and Vassilis Tsianos put it, 'Citizenship is an important tool for creating possibilities for certain groups to be included, but it can never respond to the question which migration poses to capitalist sovereignty: what about all those who are mobile and cannot be included, that is, the majority of the mobile populations.'[6]

YES – Non-reformist: Equal access to essential goods and services for all, regardless of immigration status.

In our view, a more useful demand would be to reduce the scope of immigration enforcement so far that a person would enjoy the same rights – to work, access to essential services, and so on – as a citizen or person with regular status, without having to be formally recognised as such. Framed in this way, citizenship and immigration status would no longer operate as the fulcrum on which a person's ability to enjoy their fundamental rights rests.

Demanding free, universal access to essential goods and services such as health, housing and education also breaks with the common trope that migrants are a drain on public services. As we know from the excellent campaigning for healthcare access in the UK by Docs Not Cops, this mode of campaigning also opens up space for a range of arguments. In addition to the physical and mental harms faced by people who are deterred from or unable to access healthcare, NHS charging fails on its own terms: the system costs far more to administer than it recovers, while undermining public health more broadly.

Crucially, campaigning in this vein opens up the possibility for joint action and coalition-building with broader progressive campaigns to protect and fund community access to healthcare, housing and education; after all, once the state has developed infrastructure that introduces conditionality for migrants, it is unlikely to confine conditionality to migrants alone. One need only look to some of the similarities in experience between people seeking asylum and people applying for benefits to see the same punitive operations at work. As Nicholas De Genova reminds us, 'Rather than the customary liberal plea for the belated realization of the egalitarian promises of citizenship, our greatest challenge is to cultivate a radically open-ended imagination about how to enact various forms of political struggle beyond and against the treacherous allure of citizenship.'[7]

2. Does it challenge the notion that migration harms the citizen population?

NO – Reformist: Controlling Migration Fund

The UK's Controlling Migration Fund is 'a fund to help local authorities respond to the impact of recent migration on their communities'. This fund compels local authorities to apply for scarce central government funds precisely by framing proposed initiatives in terms of alleviating pressures produced by migration and building community cohesion between migrants and minorities, on the one hand, and white Britons on the other. This Conservative policy essentially reworks and revives New Labour's Migrant Impact Fund. Both funds effectively paint migrants (and also 'ethnic minorities') as the sole or primary source of pressures on local goods and services, neatly eliding the impact of years of austerity and internal migration, and forcing local authorities to echo an anti-migrant framing in order to access funding for public services.

It may seem obvious, but it is worth reiterating that any reform that is predicated on the notion that migration harms the citizen population will be counterproductive because it operates within the logic of immigration systems, reinforcing the idea that the citizen population needs protecting, and that immigration controls are an effective way to do it.

YES – Non-reformist: End deportation post-conviction.

Deportation post-conviction is a policy in the UK whereby anyone who has been convicted of a crime and given a custodial sentence of more than twelve months must be automatically considered for deportation (very similar to deportation policies targeting 'criminal aliens' convicted of 'aggravated felonies' in the United States). Campaigning for an end to this policy is non-reformist to the extent that it breaks with the logic that foreign national offenders are a uniquely dangerous threat to society, which is a primary justification for policies of indefinite detention and deportation as banishment. This approach repositions people convicted of crimes as members of our communities who cannot simply be strategically abandoned at the convenience of the state.

3. Does it reduce the technologies, tools and tactics available for immigration control?

NO – Reformist: Use automated decisions to standardise immigration authority decision-making.

Increasing the resources available for immigration control inevitably makes the system more effective at distinguishing between different groups of people, allowing a privileged minority regular status while excluding others. Automated decision-making technology may be trained using data available from preceding immigration-enforcement practices, which in general rely on disproportionate enforcement against poor and racialised people. Automated tools simply add a technological veneer of legitimacy to the system, while doing nothing to weaken its reach into people's lives.

Reformist reforms are very often technology-focused, advocating fixes that seem to overcome human bias and rationalise processes of bureaucratic management. Such reforms prohibit one form of violence by replacing it with another. Just as the police replaced militias, and prisons replaced the gallows, the AI drone will replace the bomber pilot, the electronic tag will replace the detention cell, and virtual borders will replace the border wall – or, much more likely, new forms of high-tech bordering will supplement the old. In our times, many such reforms rely on more intensive surveillance – monitoring everyone's identity and location remotely, often through data sharing and digital infrastructure. Border abolition needs to develop a sharper analysis of how borders function in the context of big data, digital surveillance and predictive analytics.

YES – Non-reformist: Firewall essential public-service data from immigration enforcement.

On the other hand, preventing immigration enforcement from making use of data held by health, education and other agencies, such as homelessness charities, reduces its ability to trace people for detention or deportation, or to deny them access to essential services, thus diminishing the overall impact of the system on migrants and wider society.

4. Does it reduce the reach of immigration control into people's lives?

NO – Reformist: Replace detention with tagging.

This question helps us to distinguish reforms that shrink immigration control from those that merely replace or supplement it. Calls for 'alternatives to detention' that do not clearly challenge the underlying premise of detention – that migrants need to be surveilled, controlled, and ultimately removed from society – risk being co-opted by the state to justify cheaper community surveillance and control measures, such as tagging, which maintain profound restrictions on people's liberty.

YES – Non-reformist: End obligations to report to the Home Office.

By contrast, demands to end detention and obligations to report can challenge and chip away at the immigration system as a whole. We do not need to offer any alternative forms of in-community surveillance.

5. Does it reduce funding for immigration control?

NO – Reformist: More training for officials in the immigration system.

Reforms such as more training for immigration decision-makers, more staff at immigration agencies, specialist teams to deal more sensitively with specific migrant groups, and new technologies all funnel more money into the immigration system, thereby strengthening it.

YES – Non-reformist: Cut the number of immigration officials and use funds for labour-market enforcement.

Non-reformist reforms are those that direct money and resources away from the immigration system towards community practices and institutions that are more likely to safeguard people's rights. We might suggest alternative forms of state intervention that can protect the rights of all workers, such as enforcing labour market regulations – the minimum wage, for example – in ways that are always kept separate from any immigration enforcement. Firmly separating such state functions is essential to ensuring that non-citizens have recourse to the law and protection from abuse.

Where Next?

A clearer framework for differentiating reformist reforms from non-reformist ones will assist us in deciding where and how to expend our energy and resources. It will also provide a useful vocabulary for teasing out why and how particular disagreements between people and groups in migrants' rights movements emerge over strategies and specific reforms. We know from our campaigning experience that there is sometimes an assumption that everyone working on migrants' rights issues is automatically part of the same movement, and it can sometimes be difficult to articulate why some reforms differ from others. The framework of abolition – of non-reformist reforms – is therefore useful in identifying those many instances in which advocacy and campaigning diverge because different groups are working towards wholly different goals, using wholly different strategies, and – crucially – within wholly different temporalities.

An NGO that has an eighteen-month strategy to achieve a procedural tweak to the system by lobbying a small cadre of sitting politicians is not trying to do the same thing as an abolitionist campaign group that sees its task spanning generations, even if both are ostensibly working on migrants' rights. In some cases, reformist campaigns can make abolitionist work more difficult, and we should avoid expending unnecessary energy arguing with people and groups that do not share our vision. More optimistically, however, we hope that, by detailing the politics of border abolition, we might encourage NGOs to identify non-reformist reforms that can support the long-term goal of abolition, even if they do not or cannot publicly endorse abolition outright.

There is a vast array of potential non-reformist reforms that organisers might consider demanding in the here and now. Because immigration controls produce particular relationships to the state, many of them operate within specific countries: ending in-community surveillance measures like fingerprinting at university; decriminalising acts such as working, renting housing and driving, which can be integral to migrant survival; ensuring universal access to essential goods and services without any link to immigration enforcement. We should also consider reforms and practices that make removing people from the country more difficult, such as ending immigration detention, stopping mass deportation flights and ending immigration raids.

Beyond this, we need to make demands at the international level: reducing funding for international immigration enforcement measures and bodies such as Frontex – ending EU-level funding of its close neighbours for immigration enforcement infrastructure and institutions – and instead establishing global solidarity funds that increase the capacity of communities in the global South to adapt to ecological collapse. We might also look to policies that would transform relationships between countries, which have been longstanding demands of liberation movements in the global South: debt cancellation, an end to arms exports, an end to the imposition of structural adjustment measures as a condition of financial support. We should also consider bilateral and regional relaxations on immigration controls through reductions in requirements for documentation, income thresholds, and so on. Finally, we could campaign for an end to wars and quasi-wars: on terror, drugs, and so on.

What we set out above are simply some suggestions. We know that abolitionist practice is not limited to demanding non-reformist reforms; imagining and prefiguring different and better worlds and futures is just as important – which is where we direct our attention in our final chapter, or story.

Abolition is a radical orientation *and* a practical organising tool. It does not require that we have the perfect image of utopia before we get to work (although we value those who do make such sketches for us). We know that time does not progress in a regular way; history unfolds in rubato, and things speed up in times of crisis. When they do, it matters what infrastructure, relationships and alternative forms of common-sense have been developed by people who kept imagining and fighting through the hard times.[8] The point is therefore to make new things possible for those who come after us. We should build and nurture identities, relations and practices that refuse the logic of borders, and campaign for changes that will reduce their reach in the here and now. What political community will look like once we have abolished borders, and how they will be governed, remains unclear. That is okay. These are questions to be answered in the process of undoing and remaking. This is perhaps especially the case with border abolition. After all, a world without police and prisons is easier to imagine than a world without bounded political communities. Still, border abolition is our lodestar, and non-reformist reforms are some of the waypoints along the path.

INTERLUDE: FUTURES (II)

Hope is the refusal of inevitability. Even now, in times of intensifying borders, widening global inequality, climate catastrophe and technologically catalysed repression, humanity faces many possible futures. But this uncertainty can feel like a lot to hold, and our capacity to imagine better worlds risks being enveloped by all the doom and despair. When things are being taken from us – rights, protections, the promise of a future – we can end up focusing too much on short-term battles, defending a status quo that was never adequate in the first place. The suggestion that things not only might, but must be radically otherwise is most often treated with hostility and derision. We are consistently exhorted to work through procedural means towards 'realistic' or 'achievable' reforms; to follow interminable focus groups and opinion polls at the expense of imagination, hope and collective power.

What follows in this second sketch is our attempt to imagine a future radically different from our own. It is an imagined future in which life is worth living. But that does not mean life is easy. In our utopia, like in many others, threats and contestation from within and without are negotiated constantly – and where necessary, fought (a utopia of settled consensus and homogeneity would be no utopia at all). In this future, the shape of the political community is very different to our own, and a sense of openness and worldly collectivity makes the warming planet navigable. Ideas about family and kin are radically different, too, and freedom requires the right to locomotion.

A Possible Utopia

Hanna's mother is unwell, in a hospice, stable but fading. Hanna's father screened her yesterday with the news. They had known that this would happen eventually. Hanna's mother was diagnosed with lung cancer five decades ago, and while they had operated early, and she had been under the care of a specialist on an experimental and highly effective treatment regimen, it was always likely that her rest would arrive before she was able to reach her third half-century.

Hanna will need to return to London from Cagayan to be with her father in his twilight decades. His care is not her concern; he has for some years been part of the borough's Exchange, maintaining crops at the city farm and teaching children and adults his first tongue. Hanna trusts that the Exchange will ensure that he is warm and well. But when she chose him as her parent at her half-century celebration, she made a commitment to walk him to the end of his life. Still, after she spoke with him, she felt a twisting sadness in her chest. She left a note. She didn't feel like talking, and this first movement would not take long – days at most, before she came back to redistribute her possessions and say goodbye.

Flying is a mode of travel used almost exclusively in emergency. Tourist flights effectively ended when she was in her first decades; as the forest fires raged and the seas crept up, flying became more or less taboo, even before the Councils formally abolished them in climate mitigation. In any case, flying was hardly leisurely: the storms made it more dangerous, and the abrupt change in time disrupted most people's alignments for weeks. People still moved, of course, but the usual modes would have eaten into time Hanna didn't have. Bicycles and pedestrian caravans weren't worth considering for this distance, and sun-subs – deft, solar-powered amphibious craft – moved only in daylight.

At the port, Hanna asked the monitor in the wall when the next flight to London would leave, and then recorded a message for her father to let him know she was on her way. She had only flown once before, to Tijuana, when her sibling's mind had overflowed, and Civil Harm Response had asked Hanna to be part of their restoration.

Hanna was lucky – she had only five hours to wait, and the plane was already there. She stepped out onto the tarmac and greeted the guides at the entrance. 'Compassion', she said, by way of explanation. They nodded, and she sat down in a corner, stowed her bag, and leaned into memories of her mother.

Jonah and Sara rushed to watch the first SolSeed shipment come in from the South. Clouds of red dust rose as the pallets made their way down the cable-pull and fell – *whoosh* – to the ground below. For the last two months, late into the evening when the sun had finally quieted, permaculture practice in their county had been devoted to preparing the ground for what would eventually grow into their SolSeed canopy.

Great-Ma pulled out two hessian sheets from inside the top bundle and handed one to each waiting child.

SolSeed is phase two of SouthPact MITIGATE, available to inland counties not projected to warm above 42 degrees in the next five years. Sow in dry tilled soil no more than 5cm deep, chalk-water weekly and thin at one month. Your SolSeed canopy will mature at two months, reaching approximately 14 feet and reducing exterior temperatures by up to 6 degrees.

Thank you for deliberating in support of SouthPact MITIGATE and for your participation in SolSeed. Together we adapt, together we move, together we flourish.

Three months later, Sara stretched in the swaying, shaded morning, and found a message blinking on the Hub monitor. She typed in her key. The message did not have a named recipient: it was a short broadcast to the county.

Phase three movement site agreed.

Sara could not name everything she felt: relief, sadness and excitement pressed for her attention. At Council that week, they would begin deliberating on whether and when to join their scouts at the new site, or perhaps to stay and weather the changes; to try to survive adaptation and the next decade's phase four.

Sara knew why her elders had first started scouting a

movement site, although leaving must have felt unimaginable to them at the time, as it did to her now. Yet she had grown up in the shadow of this choice and so many half-shuttered homes. For as long as she could remember, the dust storms had confined them for half of every month, playing havoc with the solar cells and suffocating those animals that had failed to burrow sufficiently, or strayed too far from an open door. The sun had grown hotter and more poisonous, their dark, blistered skins demanding more and more elaborate protective creations, while the chalk-water had retreated from its usual ways and grown capricious: flood in new places, drought in old oases, and always, deeper and deeper down.

Back when SolSeed was just the half-baked source of the county technicians' unflinching disappointment, Great-Ma had explained to Sara that it was no longer certain that lands all over the earth would be able to sustain their ecosystems or their people. Councils and counties had devoted months to deliberating on the dangers, eventually forming SouthPACT MITIGATE, a programme spanning decades and so many possible futures: those where new technologies eventually undid and repaired the violence that had been wrought; others where what was lost stayed lost, but what survived was shared and not hoarded. Even before the tumult of the formal deliberations had begun, many nests in Sara's county were already half empty.

Jonah woke clammy in the dark, six months after they had stayed up into the night planting amber seeds into crumbling furrows. Hoisting himself down from the canopy platform, he settled into his chair and wheeled out under the leaves into the chirping night. The new canopy had cooled the nest and surrounding tracks, but still created too much shade above the subsistence fields for the usual crops, and the adapted seeds had not yet arrived. (SouthPact was in dispute with councils in the North, who were failing to deal with a small but disruptive guerrilla fracking campaign.) A solar cell creaked ominously. They had been hauled up to fifteen feet to overshoot the new canopy, and were more prone to cracking in the high winds. And while the cool drew the chalk-water closer to the surface of the earth, it could do nothing to temper the acidity that leached in from the remnants of the old waste sites. Yes, Sara, Jonah and all of the children in their region had grown up knowing that, if it worked, Sol-Seed would only ever be mitigation for the centuries of damage that the digging, belching extractivists had wrought. It might buy them enough time to resettle and reach phase four, but it was a bet their ancestors had hedged.

Abolitionist Futures

For all that Alberto's existence is dismal (see Interlude: Futures [I]), for us, it serves only to underline the urgency of the call for border abolition we have made in this book. The point remains that, collectively, we can act on the world. In Hanna, Jonah and Sara's world, this space for acting on the world has been expanded in many ways. Their agency – at once personal and collective – is contingent on alternative ideas about cultural difference, the planet and the family, different relationships to labour and livelihood – and, of course, the absence of undemocratic, centralised technologies designed to surveil, control and maximise industry and profit. It is no exaggeration to say Chapter 8, with its practical focus on political strategy in the present, is ultimately concerned with steering us towards their world and others like it, while preventing Alberto's from taking shape.

The future, like the present, will not be easy; but we can act now to open greater possibilities for ourselves and for those who come next. This requires dreaming and imagining, and then using these visions to orient us in the present. It requires us to think carefully about what borders do in the world now, and to seek to undermine the connected forms of violence and closure that make them seem so necessary and permanent. It means rejecting the dreary and paralysing politics of reformism, and being bold enough to say that seemingly immovable and eternal features of our world – like capitalism, prisons, war, the nuclear family and nation-states – are unjust and unsatisfying, and that we can get rid of them. It means stepping out of political abstraction and into the tumult, mess and joy of organising and campaigning, moving towards the utopias that we imagine and need, and living in ways that prefigure them. Ultimately, border abolition will be central to any revolutionary political programme – and if we cannot see that, we have already lost in the struggle to imagine liveable futures. We hope that this book can contribute to the nourishing of our varied and colourful dreams towards those better worlds.

Notes

Introduction

1. Harsha Walia's book, *Border and Rule: Global Migration, Capitalism, and the Rise of Racist Nationalism* (London: Haymarket, 2021) makes these connections skilfully in Part 4.

2. Amelia Gentleman, *The Windrush Betrayal: Exposing the Hostile Environment* (London: Guardian/Faber, 2019).

3. On everyday borders, see Nira Yuval-Davis, Georgie Wemyss and Kathryn Cassidy, *Bordering* (Oxford: Polity, 2019).

4. Catherine Dauvergne, *Making People Illegal: What Globalization Means for Migration and Law* (Cambridge: CUP, 2008).

5. On how immigration controls impact citizens and define the meanings of citizenship, see the work of Bridget Anderson – in particular, *Us and Them? The Dangerous Politics of Immigration Control* (Oxford: OUP, 2013), and '"Heads I Win. Tails You Lose." Migration and the Worker Citizen', *Current Legal Problems* 68: 1 (2015).

6. Radhika Mongia, *Indian Migration and Empire: A Colonial Genealogy of the Modern State* (Durham, NC: Duke University Press, 2018).

7. Adam McKeown, *Melancholy Order: Asian Migration and the Globalization of Borders* (New York: Columbia University Press, 2008).

8. Nadine El-Enany, *Bordering Britain: Law, Race and Empire* (Manchester: Manchester University Press, 2020).

9. Stuart Hall, *Familiar Stranger: A Life Between Two Islands* (London: Allen Lane, 2017), p. 65.

10. Angela Davis, *Are Prisons Obsolete?* (New York: Seven Stories, 2003).

11. Bridget Anderson, Nandita Sharma and Cynthia Wright, 'Editorial: Why No Borders?', *Refuge: Canada's Journal on Refugees* 26: 2 (2009), p. 6.

12. Dan Berger, Mariame Kaba and David Stein, 'What Abolitionists Do', *Jacobin*, 24 August 2017, at jacobinmag.com.

13. Ruth Wilson Gilmore, *Change Everything: Racial Capitalism and the Case for Abolition* (London: Haymarket, forthcoming).

14. E. Bloch, *The Principle of Hope* (Cambridge, MA: MIT Press, 1986 [1959]), p. 3.

15. Mariame Kaba, *We Do This 'Til We Free Us* (London: Haymarket, 2021); bell hooks, *Teaching Community: A Pedagogy of Hope* (New York: Routledge, 2003), pp. xiv–xv.

16. Les Back, 'Hope's Work', Antipode 5 (2021).

17. Kaba, *We Do This 'Til We Free Us*.

1 Race

1. David Theo Goldberg, *Are We All Postracial Yet?* (London: Polity, 2015). p. 4.

2. The phrase 'scavenger ideology' is borrowed from George L.

Mosse, *Toward the Final Solution: A History of European Racism* (New York: Howard Fertig, 1978).

3. Bridget Anderson, *Us and Them? The Dangerous Politics of Immigration Control* (Oxford: OUP, 2013).

4. David Theo Goldberg, *The Threat of Race: Reflections on Racial Neoliberalism* (London: Wiley-Blackwell, 2009), pp. 1–32.

5. Walter D. Mignolo, *The Darker Side of Western Modernity: Global Futures, Decolonial Options* (Durham, NC: Duke University Press, 2011).

6. Sivamohan Valluvan, *The Clamour of Nationalism: Race and Nation in Twenty-First-Century Britain* (Manchester: Manchester University Press, 2019), p. 54.

7. Etienne Balibar, 'Racism and Nationalism', in E. Balibar and I. Wallerstein, eds, *Race, Nation, Class: Ambiguous Identities* (London: Verso, 1991), p. 48.

8. Hagar Kotef, *Movement and the Ordering of Freedom: On Liberal Governances of Mobility* (Durham, NC: Duke University Press, 2015), p. 15.

9. James C. Scott, *Seeing Like a State: How Certain Schemes to Improve the Human Condition Have Failed* (New Haven, CT: Yale University Press, 1999).

10. Nandita Sharma, *Home Rule: National Sovereignty and the Separation of Natives and Migrants* (Durham, NC: Duke University Press, 2020); Aderanti Adepoju, 'Illegals and Expulsion in Africa: The Nigerian Experience', *International Migration Review* 18: 3 (1984); Mahmood Mamdani, *Neither Settler Nor Native: The Making and Unmaking of Permanent Minorities* (Cambridge, MA: Harvard University Press, 2020).

11. Mahmood Mamdani, *Define and Rule: Native as Political Identity* (The W. E. B. Du Bois Lectures) (Cambridge, MA: Harvard University Press, 2012).

12. Achille Mbembe, 'The Idea of a Borderless World', *Africa Is a Country*, 2019, at africasacountry.com.

2 Gender

1. Bridget Anderson, *Us and Them? The Dangerous Politics of Immigration control* (Oxford: OUP, 2013), p. 66.

2. Ibid., p. 67

3. Eithné Luibhéid, *Pregnant on Arrival: Making the Illegal Immigrant* (Minneapolis, MN: University of Minnesota Press, 2013).

4. Luke de Noronha, 'No Tears Left to Cry: Being Deported Is a Distressing Nightmare', *VICE News*, 1 December 2016, at vice.com.

5. United Nations, *Universal Declaration of Human Rights* (1948).

6. Council of Europe, *The European Convention on Human Rights* (Strasbourg: Directorate of Information, 1952).

7. Silvia Federici, *Wages Against Housework* (Bristol: Falling Wall, 1975).

8. Anderson *Us and Them?*, pp. 166–7.

9. Ibid., pp. 172–6.

10. Juno Mac and Molly Smith, *Revolting Prostitutes: The Fight for Sex Workers' Rights* (London: Verso, 2018).

11. Julia O'Connell Davidson, *Modern Slavery: The Margins of Freedom* (Basingstoke: Palgrave Macmillan, 2015).

12. See Detained Voices for the record of these demands: detainedvoices.com.

13. Anderson, *Us and Them?*, p. 137.

14. Ava Caradonna, 'We Speak but You Don't Listen: Migrant Sex Worker Organising at the Border', *X:talk Project* (2016), at opendemocracy.net.

15. 'bell hooks – Are You Still a Slave? Liberating the Black Female Body', YouTube, 7 May 2014, accessed 28 April 2022.

3 Capitalism

1. Harsha Walia describes this broad relationship between dispossession, containment and the importation of temporary and illegalised labour in terms of 'border imperialism'. Harsha Walia, *Undoing Border Imperialism* (Oakland, CA: AK Press, 2013).

2. Ruth Wilson Gilmore, 'Abolition Geography and the Problem of Innocence', in G. T. Johnson and A. Loubin, eds, *Futures of Black Radicalism* (New York: Verso, 2017).

3. Lisa O'Carroll, 'Immigration Raid on Byron Hamburgers Rounds up 35 Workers', *Guardian*, 27 July 2016.

4. Alberto Toscano, 'Dirty deportation tactics at Soas', *Guardian*, 17 June 2009.

5. Nicholas De Genova describes this as the 'condition of deportability'. Nicholas De Genova, 'Migrant "Illegality" and Deportability in Everyday Life', *Annual Review of Anthropology* 31 (2002).

6. See 'Grunwick 40: Remembering the Grunwick Strike 40 Years On', at grunwick40.wordpress.com.

7. For a damning critique of Len McCluskey's interventions, see Ewa Jasiewicz, 'I Am a Union Organiser. Len McCluskey's Migrant Clampdown Will Only Benefit Bosses', *Guardian*, 15 November 2019.

8. Vernon M. Briggs, Jr., *Immigration and American Unionism* (Ithaca, NY: Cornell University Press, 2001).

9. Mike Elk 'Undocumented Workers Find New Ally as Unions Act to Halt Deportations', *Guardian*, 22 March 2018

10. Josh Eidelson, 'Unions are training hotel workers to face down immigration raids' *Bloomberg Online*, 20 September 2017.

11. AFL-CIO, 'Iced Out: How Immigration Enforcement Has Interfered With Workers Rights', ecommons.cornell.edu, 2009.

12. Dan Berger, Mariame Kaba and David Stein. 'What Abolitionists Do', *Jacobin*, 24 August 2017, at jacobinmag.com.

13. 'Interview: Bridget Anderson on Europe's "Violent Humanitarianism" in the Mediterranean', *Ceasefire*, at ceasefiremagazine.co.uk.

14. On migration and existential mobility, see Ghassan Hage, 'A Not So Multi-Sited Ethnography of a Not So Imagined Community', *Anthropological Theory* 5: 4 (2005).

15. Todd Miller, *Empire of Borders: The Expansion of the US Border Around the World* (London: Verso, 2019); Adrian Little and Nick Vaughan-Williams 'Stopping Boats, Saving Lives, Securing Subjects: Humanitarian Borders in Europe and Australia', *European Journal of International Relations* 23: 3 (2017).

16. Achille Mbembe, 'The Idea of a Borderless World', *Africa Is a Country*, 2019, at africasacountry.com.

17. Walia, *Undoing Border Imperialism*.

18. William Walters 'Acts of Demonstration: Mapping the Territory of (Non-)Citizenship', in E. Isin and G. Neilson, eds, *Acts of Citizenship* (London: Zed, 2008)

19. *The Communist Manifesto*, after all, calls for the abolition of private property, of bourgeois individuality, of the family, *and* of countries and nationality.

4 Policing

1. On Operation Nexus and deportation on the basis of 'non-convictions', see Luqmani Thompson & Partners, 'Operation Nexus: briefing paper', 2014 luqmanithompson.com; Frances Webber, 'Deportation on Suspicion', Institute for Race Relations, 20 June 2013, at irr.org.uk, and Melanie Griffiths, 'Foreign, Criminal: A Doubly Damned Modern British Folk-Devil', *Citizenship Studies* 21 (2017). For more on the stories of Darel and others deported to Jamaica, see Luke de Noronha, *Deporting Black Britons: Portraits of Deportation to Jamaica* (Manchester: Manchester University Press, 2020).

2. On the criminalisation of migration, see Katja Aas and Mary Bosworth, eds, *The Borders of Punishment: Migration, Citizenship, and Social Exclusion* (Oxford: OUP, 2013); Juliet Stumpf, 'The Crimmigration Crisis: Immigrants, Crime, and Sovereign Power', *American University Law Review* 56: 2 (2006).

3. Jenna Loyd, Matt Mitchelson and Andrew Burridge, eds, *Beyond Walls and Cages: Prisons, Borders, and Global Crisis* (Athens, GA: University of Georgia Press, 2012).

4. Paul Gilroy, 'The myth of black criminality', in *Socialist Register* (London: Merlin Press, 1982), pp. 47–56.

5. This closely mirrors the Illegal Immigration Reform and Immigrant Responsibility Act of 1996 in the US – although without its retroactive force, and with slightly better human-rights provisions.

6. Emma Kaufman, *Punish and Expel: Border Control, Nationalism, and the New Purpose of the Prison* (Oxford: OUP, 2015); Alpa Parmar, 'Policing Belonging: Race and Nation in the UK', in Mary Bosworth, Alpa Parmar and Yolanda Vazquez, eds, *Race, Criminal Justice and Migration Control: Enforcing the Boundaries of Belonging* (Oxford: OUP, 2018).

7. Ruth Wilson Gilmore, 'Race, Capitalism, Abolitionism', in Loyd, Mitchelson and Burridge, *Beyond Walls and Cages*.

8. 'Home Secretary: Backing the Bill on illegal immigration', conservatives.com, 8 December 2021.

9. Angela Davis, *Are Prisons Obsolete?* (New York: Seven Stories, 2003).

10. Jackie Wang, *Carceral Capitalism* (Cambridge, MA: MIT Press, 2018).

11. Gilmore, 'Race, Capitalism, Abolitionism'.

12. Luke de Noronha, *Deporting Black Britons: Portraits of Deportation to Jamaica* (Manchester: Manchester University Press, 2020).

5 Counter-terror

1. Anthony Loyd, 'Shamima Begum: the interview in full', *The Times*, 14 February 2019.

2. Arun Kundnani, *The Muslims Are Coming! Islamophobia, Extremism, and the Domestic War on Terror* (London: Verso, 2014).

3. Nisha Kapoor, *Deport, Deprive, Extradite: 21st Century State Extremism* (London: Verso, 2018).

4. M. Longo, *The Politics of Borders: Sovereignty, Security, and the Citizen after 9/11* (Cambridge: CUP, 2017).

5. Kapoor, *Deport, Deprive, Extradite*.

6. Most deprivations have occurred when individuals are out of the country, and some men – such as Bilal al-Berjawi and Mohamed Sakr – were deprived of their citizenship before being killed by US drones. In the case of Pham Minh, the courts argued that he was still a Vietnamese citizen even though the Vietnamese state did not recognise him as such, and he was subsequently extradited to the United States. At a similar time, Hilal al-Jedda managed to win his case on appeal against deprivation, arguing that he could not simply reapply for Iraqi citizenship, as the home secretary claimed. However, the al-Jedda case served as proof of the need to revise the law further, resulting in the extension of powers in the Immigration Act 2014 that would later support Shamima Begum's denationalisation.

7. *Aziz and Ors v Secretary of State for the Home Department*, EWCA Civ 1884 (8 August 2018).

8. Nisha Kapoor and Kasia Narkowicz, 'Unmaking Citizens: Passport Removals, Pre-emptive Policing and the Reimagining of Colonial Governmentalities', *Ethnic and Racial Studies* 42:16 (2019).

9. Gareth Peirce, 'Was It Like This for the Irish?', *London Review of Books*, 10 April 2008.

10. Kapoor, *Deport, Deprive, Extradite*.

11. Home Office, *CONTEST: The United Kingdom's Strategy for Countering Terrorism* (London: Home Office, 2011).

12. Home Office, *Prevent Strategy* (London: Home Office, 2011).

13. Section 26 of the Counter-Terrorism and Security Act 2015

14. Home Office, *Prevent Strategy*.

15. Police officers have sought powers to criminalise so-called 'gang members' for inciting serious violence without having to prove that their social media posts or music videos are directly linked to any actual acts of violence, and terrorism laws have provided some inspiration to this effort.

16. Anthony Loyd, 'Shamima Begum: the interview in full', *The Times*, 14 February 2019.

17. Bridget Anderson, '"Heads I Win. Tails You Lose." Migration and the Worker Citizen', *Current Legal Problems* 68: 1 (2015).

18. Nandita Sharma, *Home Rule: National Sovereignty and the Separation of Natives and Migrants* (Durham, NC: Duke University Press, 2020).

19. Mahmood Mamdani, *Neither Settler Nor Native: The Making and Unmaking of Permanent Minorities* (Cambridge, MA: Harvard University Press, 2020).

6 Databases

1. Amelia Gentleman, *The Windrush Betrayal: Exposing the Hostile Environment* (London: Guardian/Faber, 2019).

2. David Goodhart and Richard Norrie, 'The UK Border Audit: Is the UK Border Now Fit for Purpose? A Post-Windrush Review', *Policy Exchange*, 2018, at policyexchange.org.uk.

3. 'Taking the Initiative Party', at theinitiativeparty.org.uk.

4. James C. Scott, *Seeing Like a State: How Certain Schemes for Improving the Human Condition Have Failed* (New Haven, CT: Yale University Press, 1998).

5. Jane Caplan and John Torpey, eds, *Documenting Individual Identity* (Oxford: Princeton University Press, 2018).

6. John Torpey, *The Invention of the Passport: Surveillance, Citizenship and the State* (Cambridge: CUP, 2000).

7. Simone Browne, *Dark Matters: On the Surveillance of Blackness* (Durham, NC: Duke University Press, 2015); Keith Breckenbridge, *Biometric State: The Global Politics of Identification and Surveillance in South Africa, 1850 to the Present* (Cambridge: CUP, 2014); Chandak Sengoopta, *Imprint of the Raj: How Fingerprinting Was Born in Colonial India* (Basingstoke: Pan MacMillan, 2003).

8. Jon Agar, 'Modern Horrors: British Identity and Identity Cards', in Caplan and Torpey, *Documenting Individual Identity*.

9. George Grylls, 'Digital "ID Cards" lead the Dominic Cummings data revolution', *The Times,* 2 September 2020.

10. Elections Bill, House of Commons Session 2021–22.

11. Statewatch, 'Data Protection, Immigration Enforcement and Fundamental Rights: What the EU's Regulations on Interoperability Mean for People with Irregular Status', *Center for European Policy Studies (CEPS) and European Migration Law* (Statewatch, 2019), p. 8.

12. Privacy International, 'Home Office Biometrics (HOB) Programme Brief', August 2019.

13. Statewatch, 'Data Protection, Immigration Enforcement and Fundamental Rights, p. 4.

14. See nidsfacts.com, accessed 24 December 2021.

15. See, for example, Oxfam, 'The EU Trust Fund for Africa: Trapped Between Aid Policy and Migration Politics', Briefing Paper, January 2020.

16. See id4d.worldbank.org/, accessed 24 December 2021

17. M. Latonero, 'Stop Surveillance Humanitarianism', *New York Times*, 11 July 2019.

18. '(1977) The Combahee River Collective Statement', at blackpast.org.

19. Combahee River Collective, 'The Combahee River Collective: A Black Feminist Statement', *Capitalist Patriarchy and the Case for Socialist Feminism*, Zillah R. Eisenstein (ed.) (New York: Monthly Review Press, 1979), pp. 362–72.

20. Stuart Hall, 'New Ethnicities', in J. Donald and A. Rattansi, eds, *Race, Culture and Difference* (London: Sage, 1992).

7 Algorithms

1. Stephan Scheel, 'Recuperation through Crisis Talk', *South Atlantic Quarterly* 117: 2 (2018), pp. 267–89.

2. See roborder.eu, accessed 24 December 2021.

3. Zach Campbell, 'Swarms of Drones, Piloted by Artificial Intelligence, May Soon Patrol Europe's Borders', *Intercept*, 11 May 2019, at theintercept.com.

4. Statewatch, 'EU Pays for "Watch Towers" for Guarding the Georgia–Turkey Border', 24 April 2017, at statewatch.org.

5. Russell Brandom, 'The US Border Patrol Is Trying to Build Face-Reading Drones', *The Verge*, 6 April 2017, at theverge.com.

6. See 'Anduril: Our Work', at anduril.com.

7. European Commission, 'Smart lie-detection system to tighten EU's busy borders', ec.europa.eu, 24 October 2018.

8. Sebastsien Klovig Skelton, 'UK Facial Recognition Project to Identify Hidden Faces', *Computer Weekly*, 18 March 2020, at computerweekly.com.

9. Louise Amoore, *The Politics of Possibility: Risk and Security Beyond Probability* (Durham, NC: Duke University Press, 2013), p. 193.

10. Annie Jacobsen, *First Platoon: A Story of Modern War in the Age of Identity Dominance* (Boston, MA: Dutton, 2021).

11. Ken Klippenstein and Sara Sirota, 'The Taliban Have Seized US Military Biometrics Devices', *Intercept*, 17 August 2021, at theintercept.com.

12. Privacy International, 'Biometrics Collection under the Pretext of Counter-Terrorism', 28 May 2021, at privacyinternational.org.

13. Chris Jones, 'Automated Suspicion: The EU's New Travel Surveillance Initiatives', Statewatch, 2020, pdf available at statewatch.org.

14. Felipe De La Hoz, 'DHS Plans to Start Collecting Eye Scans and DNA — With the Help of Defense Contractors', *Intercept*, 17 November 2020, at theintercept.com.

15. See the excellent reports by the migrant justice organisation Mijente: 'Who's Behind ICE: The Tech and Data Companies Fuelling Deportation' (2018) and 'The War Against Immigrants: Trump's Tech Tools Powered by Palantir' (2019), both available in pdf at mijente.net.

16. Todd Miller, 'More than a Wall: Corporate Profiteering and the Militarization of US Borders', Transnational Institute, September 2019, at tni.org.

17. Amoore, *Politics of Possibility*.

18. Palantir worked first with the US military from 2009 onwards, providing software to help predict the location of IEDs in Afghanistan and Iraq, before moving into predictive policing in 2012. This was trialled first in New Orleans, which gathered vast amounts of data on individuals and their associations to identify potential victims and perpetrators of violence, who could then be 'invited' to join the city's CeaseFire programme. See Sharon Weinberger, 'Techie Software Soldier Spy', *New York Magazine*, 28 September 2020.

19. Petra Molnar and Lex Gill, 'Bots at the Gate: A Human Rights Analysis of Automated Decision-Making in Canada's Immigration and Refugee System', University of Toronto International Human Rights Program and the Citizen Lab, Munk School of Global Affairs, 2018, pdf available at citizenlab.ca.

20. Louise Amoore, *Cloud Ethics: Algorithms and the Attributes of*

Ourselves and Others (Durham, NC: Duke University Press, 2020).

21. Tendayi Achiume has made similar arguments in her investigations into new technologies, border-maintenance and racial discrimination. See, for example, her 'Report of the Current Special Rapporteur on Contemporary Forms of Racism, Racial Discrimination, Xenophobia and Related Intolerance', at citizenlab.ca – submitted to the 75th session of the Office of the United Nations High Commissioner for Human Rights, November 2020.

22. *Jacobin*, 'Unionizing Google Workers: We Want Democracy at Work', 13 January 2021, at jacobinmag.com.

23. Michel Foucault, *Security, Territory, Population: Lectures at the Collège de France, 1977–78* (Basingstoke: Palgrave Macmillan, 2007).

24. Amoore, *Cloud Ethics*.

8 Abolition

1. Mariame Kaba, *We Do This 'Til We Free Us* (London: Haymarket, 2021), p.2.

2. Dan Berger, Mariame Kaba and David Stein. 'What Abolitionists Do', *Jacobin*, 24 August 2017, at jacobinmag.com.

3. André Gorz, *Strategy for Labor: A Radical Proposal* (Boston, MA: Beacon, 1967), pp. 7–8.

4. Critical Resistance. 'What Is Abolition?', available at critical resistance.org, accessed 24 December 2021.

5. See *Critical Resistance*, 'Reformist Reforms vs. Abolitionist Steps to End IMPRISONMENT', available at, criticalresistance.org, accessed 24 December 2021; and Mariame Kaba, 'Police "Reforms" You Should Always Oppose', *TruthOut*, 7 December 2014, truthout.org, accessed 24 December 2021.

6. Dimitris Papadopoulos and Vassilis S. Tsianos, 'After Citizenship:

Autonomy of Migration, Organisational Ontology and Mobile Commons', *Citizenship Studies* 17: 2 (2013), p. 184.

7. Nicholas De Genova, 'Citizenship', in Deborah R. Vargas, Lawrence La Fountain-Stokes and Nancy Raquel Mirabal, eds, *Keywords for Latina/o Studies* (New York, NY: New York University Press, 2017).

8. Yes, we know we are basically paraphrasing Milton Friedman here. Whoops!